DATE DUE			

BOOM TOWN GROWTH MANAGEMENT:
A Case Study of Rock Springs— Green River, Wyoming

John S. Gilmore and Mary K. Duff
University of Denver Research Institute

•WESTVIEW PRESS•BOULDER•COLORADO•

Published in 1975 in the United States of America
by Westview Press, Inc.
  1898 Flatiron Court
  Boulder, Colorado 80301
  Frederick A. Praeger, Publisher and Editorial Director

Library of Congress Cataloging in Publication Data

Gilmore, John S
    Boom town growth management.

    1. Municipal services—Green River, Wyo.
2. Green River, Wyo.—Economic conditions.
I. Duff, Mary K., joint author. II. Title.
HD4606.G68G53   309.2'62   75-25905
ISBN 0-89158-010-7

Printed and bound in the United States of America

This book is based on research sponsored by the Rocky Mountain Energy Company, in the belief that effective solutions to these and similar impact problems can come only with broad understanding of their nature.

The conduct of the research was solely in the hands of the authors, John S. Gilmore and Mary K. Duff of the University of Denver Research Institute. The findings and recommendations are those of the authors.

CONTENTS

Page

LIST OF TABLES AND FIGURES   ix

Chapter

1. SWEETWATER COUNTY: PAST, PRESENT AND FUTURE   1

    Before the Boom   1
    The Impact of the Boom   2
    Where the Boom Came From and Where It Is
      Going   2

2. THE BOOM PROBLEMS   10

    The Quality of Life Has Been Degraded   10
    Industrial Productivity and Profitability
      Have Declined   15
    The Viability of Municipal Government is
      Uncertain   15
    The Present Environment for Problem Solving   19
    The Issues Raised by Boom Growth   20

3. THE PROBLEM TRIANGLE   22

    Interdependence of the Problems   23
    Changing the Means of Handling Growth   24

4. THE GROWTH PROCESSES   26

    The Market Mechanisms   26
    The Stable Situation   27
    The Effects of Major Increases in Basic
      Plant Investment   29

5. BOOM TOWN GROWTH MANAGEMENT   35

    Growth Management Functions   36
    Function 1: Balancing Basic and Induced
      Capital Investment   36
    Function 2: Affecting Resource Use and
      Conservation   40

Chapter   Page

    Function 3: Developing Labor Force   41
    Function 4: Accommodating and Retaining
      Population   42

6. A HIERARCHY OF OBJECTIVES LEADING TO PROGRAM
    PACKAGES AND A DECISION AGENDA   44

    Objectives   44
    The Hierarchy   45
    Detailed Operational Objectives   49
    Program Package   52
    Housing Program Package in Response to
      Detailed Operational Objective No. 2   52
    Housing Program Package Financial Notes   54
    Program Package to Enhance the Intangible
      Aspects of Quality of Life in Response
      to Detailed Operational Objectives 8 and 9   56
    Enhancing the Intangible Aspects of the
      Quality of Life--Financial Notes   62
    The Agenda   63

Appendixes

A. CONCEPTS AND REMEDIES   71

    The Priorities Board (The Ferrero Plan)   71
    Housing and Public Facilities: A Wyoming
      Development Corporation   73
    A Greater Capability for Growth Management   76
    Specific Remedies   78

        Assumptions on Population Forecasts,
        Housing, and Schoolroom Requirements   81

        Possible Areas for Industry Support
        of Local Government   83

    Category I Topics--Lobbying   83
    Category II Items--Financial Support   84
    Status of Local Government Wants   87

B. THE RESIDENTS OF SWEETWATER COUNTY, WYOMING:
    A NEEDS ASSESSMENT SURVEY   89

    Introduction   89
    Summary and Conclusions   90
    Methodology   92
    The Demography of Sweetwater County   98

Appendixes   Page

    Marital Status   98
    Size of Household   98
    Mobility Patterns   98
    Education   99
    Income   99

        Employment Patterns   101

    Place of Employment   101
    Evaluation of Employment Opportunities in
      Sweetwater County   103
    Future Employment Expectations   104

        Problem Areas and Priorities   105

    Major Problem Areas   106
    Perceived Solutions to Major Problems   111
    Direction in Which the Community is Seen
      as Moving   112
    Most Rewarding Aspects of Life in the Area   114
    Evaluation of the Importance of Specific
      Community Services   116
    Comparison of Services Offered in Sweetwater
      County with Those Offered Elsewhere in the
      Country   121
    Used Local Services   124
    Suggested Ways in Which Local Services Could
      Be Improved   125

        The Mood of Sweetwater County   130

    Job Satisfaction   130
    Level of Satisfaction with Present Living
      Quarters   131
    Satisfaction with Family Life   132
    Desire to Remain in the Area   132

        Present Dwelling Patterns   134

    Description of Present Home   134
    Housing Costs   138
    Initial Difficulties in Finding Housing   138
    Evaluation of Present Housing   138

        Desired Housing Conditions   140

    Description of Ideal Home   140

Appendixes   Page

    Cost Considerations   141
    Choices Among Housing Alternatives   142

        Residents' Life Styles   145

    Activities Engaged In   145
    Interest in Adult and Vocational Education
      Courses   147
    Commitment to Community   148

        Needs Assessment Survey Questionnaire   151

        Pictures of Typical Sweetwater County,
        Housing Units   177

Table   Page

    I   Sweetwater County Employment Estimates
        and Forecasts   4

   II   Population Growth Rates   8

  III   Forecasts of Population, Families, School
        Children, Schoolrooms, and Housing Units
        Need for Sweetwater County to the Early
        1980s   9

   IV   Population and Assessed Valuation   16

    V   Roles in Growth Management Activities   46

  A-I   Concepts vs. Issues   78

  B-I   Sample Subgroup Sizes   95

 B-II   Clusters of Respondents by Employment and
        Length of Residence Categories and Distri-
        bution of Housing Arrangements for Each
        Cluster   96

B-III   Employment, Housing Type, and Length of
        Residence in County by Location of
        Residence   97

 B-IV   Demographic Characteristics   100

  B-V   Occupation and Place of Employment of
        Head of Household   101

 B-VI   Length of Employment   102

B-VII   Expectations for Leaving the Area   105

B-VIII Major Problem Areas by Location of
        Residence   108

 B-IX   Direction Community is Moving   113

ix

Table   Page

     B-X   Priorities for Problem Solution   119

    B-XI   Priority of Services--Newcomers   121

   B-XII   Comparison of Services; Sweetwater County
            Versus Preferred Location Elsewhere   123

  B-XIII   Median Distance to Most Frequently Used
            Services (Miles)   125

   B-XIV   Indices of Satisfaction   133

    B-XV   Type of Dwelling Unit   135

   B-XVI   Demographic Characteristics of Residents
            of Various Types of Dwelling Units   136

  B-XVII   Advantages of Present Home   139

 B-XVIII   Housing Characteristics Desired   142

   B-XIX   Ratings of Housing Alternatives   144

    B-XX   Top Ten Activities   146

   B-XXI   Ten Most Enjoyable Activities   146

  B-XXII   Degree of Fit with Statements Describing
            Various Social Activities   149

Figure

      1   Sweetwater County Population Forecasts   7

      2   Community Growth Model: The Stable
           Situation   28

      3   Community Growth Model: Incremental
           Change, Balanced Growth   30

      4   Community Growth Model: Unbalanced
           Growth   33

      5   Community Growth Model: Growth Management
           Functions   37

BEFORE THE BOOM

From the late 1800s railroading and coal mining have been
the mainstays of the Sweetwater County, Wyoming economy.
The Union Pacific Railroad still has its southwestern Wyoming yards at Green River. In the days of steam, the
Rock Springs coal mines fueled almost the entire road.

Agriculture was always limited by the arid climate. Sheep
grazing has dominated the sparse ranching activity
throughout this century.

After World War II, local railroad employment followed
the national pattern of decline. About 1,700 were so employed in 1950, 600 in 1956, and less than 300 today.
Similarly, coal mining employed over 2,000 in 1950, and
has declined to negligible numbers today. Ranching currently employs slightly more than 200 people.

As the traditional industries almost died away, others
took their place. Coal mining dropped off in the late
1950s when the Union Pacific Railroad completed diesel-
izing its motive power, but the U.S. Bureau of Reclamation
built the Flaming Gorge Dam--a massive construction project. Trona mining, a natural source of the industrial
chemical soda ash, grew steadily during the 1960s. Oil
and gas production also expanded.

In 1970, trona mining was the mainstay of the economy and
the railroad was still an important employer. A well-
developed local services sector of the economy existed,
with an estimated 1.7 local service employees for every
basic employee.*

---

*Local service employment is that supported by trans-
actions between firms and residents within the region; it
is generated by basic employment--that supported by trans-

In 1971, current economic growth started to accelerate.
By 1973, a boom had hit Sweetwater County, and by 1974
there was widespread awareness of its impact.

The county population in 1970 was 18,391; by the end of
1974, it was estimated at 36,900--reflecting an annual
growth rate of 19 percent. Five percent is generally
about as much growth as a small community can comfortably
absorb.

By now, no one can ignore the boom and the problems it
brings.

1. *The quality of life deteriorated* as growth in basic
   industry outran the local service sector's ability
   to provide housing, health services, schooling, retailing, and urban services. As the county population doubled in that time, the many newcomers were
   not satisfactorily integrated into the community.

2. *Industrial productivity declined 25 to 40 percent* in
   mining because of labor turnover and labor shortages.
   Construction productivity declined, and the local
   services sector also suffered. The quality of life
   problems were the basic cause of this. Job satisfaction is high, but many of the newcomers necessary
   for industrial growth are sufficiently dissatisfied
   with life in Sweetwater County to consider leaving.

3. *The local services sector failed to meet the needs*
   of the community for goods and services. Capital
   investment in the local services sector--both local
   government and commercial activity--did not build up
   adequately, nor did local government revenues.

WHERE THE BOOM CAME FROM AND WHERE IT IS GOING

The Sweetwater County boom is the cumulative result of
separate corporate decisions to invest large amounts of
capital in new construction and expanded operations in
Sweetwater County during the early 1970s. Probably no
single person or organization was aware of all of these
decisions. Certainly no one anticipated the consequence
that all would interact, each construction project making
the others more difficult, and all of them adding to the
load placed on the community's capabilities.

---

actions which export goods and services outside the region
and, in turn, import purchasing power. The estimated
breakdown of employment between basic and local service
employment is shown in Table I, page 4.

Specifically these decisions led to massive increases in
construction employment, building the Jim Bridger Power
Plant and expanding trona plant and mining operations.
Construction employment in the county was about 400 in
1970; it is about 4,800 in 1974. In the same four years,
mining and processing employment (mostly trona, but some
oil and gas) went from about 1,500 to over 2,600.

These employment increases, in turn, led to attempts by
local trade, service, and governmental entities to add to
their work forces to serve the needs created by the capital spending boom. As a result, total employment in the
county doubled in four years (from about 7,000 to almost
15,000), and is still growing as the local service sector
struggles to catch up with the demand. These changes are
detailed in Table I. The specific assumptions underlying
the forecasts of future employment are spelled out in the
accompanying notes. The context for these assumptions is
described below.

The boom is going to continue. It may level off: the
growth rate is dropping, but growth itself goes on. As
shown in Table I, employment will probably grow at a 4-8
percent annual rate between now and 1978.

Employment will continue to grow into the early 1980s,
probably accelerating after 1978. It could double again
between 1978 and the early 1980s, involving a return to
boom growth rates. Alternatively, a very conservative
forecast indicates a lower percent growth rate from 1978
into the early 1980s, a rate permitting some catching up
in public facilities and housing.

   The basis for growth. These Sweetwater County growth
expectations are based primarily on strong market prospects for soda ash and coal in the United States. In the
past, the greater part of U.S. soda ash production was
synthesized through the Solvay process, a method that
produces water polluting effluents. Some Solvay plants
have already been closed, and others may shut down in
years to come. At the same time, domestic and foreign demand for soda ash is growing. It is estimated that the
demand for natural (nonsynthetic) soda ash will double by
1985. It is further believed that most of this increased
supply will come from trona mines in southwest Wyoming--
particularly from Sweetwater County.*

Currently, the rate of coal production in the United
States is about 600 million tons per year. Planning for
Project Independence, the move toward U.S. energy self-

_____

   *Based on confidential interviews with trona pro-
ducing companies.

3

TABLE I

Sweetwater County Employment Estimates and Forecasts

	1970[a]	1972[a]	1974	1978 Conservative	1978 High	Early 1980s 1982? Conservative	1982 Moderate	1982 High
Agriculture	230	230	230	220	220	200	200	200
Mining and processing (including trona, oil, and coal)	1,530	2,020	2,650	4,300	4,400	7,000	8,500	10,000
Construction (basic)	--	1,300	4,200	1,600[b]	3,600	1,000	4,000	5,000
Power plants	--	--	100	150	175	300	400	700
Federal government	160	170	170	180	200	250	250	300
Railroad (includes layovers)	500	350	350	350	350	200	400	400
Miscellaneous (trade x .1 plus services x .2)	330	400	525	650	700	850	1,200	1,400
Total Basic Employment	2,750	4,470	8,225	7,450	9,645	9,800	14,950	18,000
Construction (local service)	370	405	700	--	--	--	--	--
Transportation, communication, and utilities	420	440	650	--	--	--	--	--
Trade x .9	1,230	1,550	2,000	--	--	--	--	--
Services x .8	750	900	1,200	--	--	--	--	--
State and local government (including education)	880	1,185	1,300	--	--	--	--	--
Finance, insurance, and real estate	150	165	200	--	--	--	--	--
Miscellaneous	680	890	950	--	--	--	--	--
Total Local Service Employment	4,480	5,535	7,000	8,940	10,600	11,760	16,450	18,000
Basic to Local Service Multiplier	1.6	1.2	.9	1.2	1.1	1.2	1.1	1.0
TOTAL EMPLOYMENT	7,230	10,005	15,225	16,390	20,245	21,560	31,400	36,000

4

a1970 and 1972 employment figures are estimated from U.S. Census and Wyoming Employment Security Commission data; multipliers are calculated from these. Figures for 1974 and subsequent figures are DRI estimates based on employer interviews and DRI staff judgments; multipliers were estimated by DRI staff.

bThe continuation of the Jim Bridger Plant construction will add to the 1978 construction employment figures by about 1000 in total employment; population (Figure 1) for 1978 Conservative will increase by 3000. This recently announced change is not reflected elsewhere in this book.

The Assumptions Underlying Employment Forecasts: Notes to Table I

1978 Conservative

Assumes a sharp drop in construction employment after completion of Jim Bridger Unit #4.

Assumes the presently programmed expansion of existing trona production (including Texasgulf) and entry of a new major producer, e.g., Diamond Alkali, Olin Mathieson, into plant construction with production to follow.

Assumes the present level of oil activity and only the Stansbury coal mine to be in production.

1978 High

Assumes that construction will continue on additional units and transmission facilities at Jim Bridger Plant.

Assumes some additional increase in coal or oil employment.

Early 1980s Low

Assumes continued expansion of trona producers already identified.
Assumes no growth in oil and gas; some growth in coal employment.
Assumes no major construction of mining or industrial facilities.

Early 1980s Moderate

Similar to low estimates, but assumes construction of one major coal gasification or liquefaction plant, plus some power plant construction.

Early 1980s High

Similar to moderate, but assumes intensive coal development and some oil shale development. No provision is made for entry of entire new industries, such as manufacturing of glass or steel. There is also no provision made for the removal of any existing industrial processes, e.g., if liquid trona solution or slurry were to be transported elsewhere by pipeline, some assumed trona processing employment might be eliminated. In situ processing of trona or coal might further reduce estimated employment, but neither is considered likely within the next ten years.

sufficiency, anticipates increasing coal production to somewhere between 1.2 billion tons and 1.5 billion tons within ten years. Much of this is for electric generation, some for coal gasification or liquefaction. Accomplishing this will require opening new U.S. mines at the rate of one large new surface mine and one new underground mine monthly, throughout the next decade. Given Sweetwater County's reserves of coal and access to water, it is believed that coal development in the county will occur at an accelerating rate, and that some form of coal processing will eventually take place.

Sweetwater County also has extensive oil shale reserves. Most of them are too deep for ready access by conventional mining processes. Thus, their development will probably not occur until *in situ* processing is feasible. Project Independence research funds, as well as oil industry efforts, are being committed to this, so oil shale development in Sweetwater County will be a strong possibility in the early 1980s.

None of these forecasts indicates that Sweetwater County's economic growth is over.

Population growth. In fact, population will continue to grow, based on the additional employment. The recent history of population growth and the forecast into the early 1980s is shown in Figure 1.

The forecasted population growth rates are shown in Table II. As mentioned earlier, a five percent growth rate is about all that a small community can absorb.

The composition of this growth and some of its implications for housing and school requirements are summarized in Table III.

---

*The assumptions for these estimates are detailed in Appendix A.

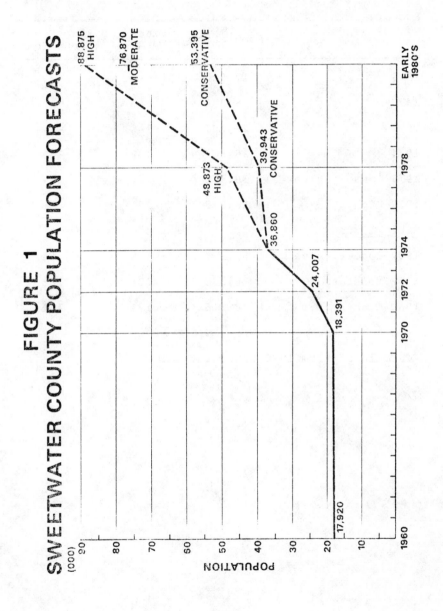

FIGURE 1
SWEETWATER COUNTY POPULATION FORECASTS

TABLE II

Population Growth Rates

	Population	Since 1970	During Previous Four Years
1960	17,920	--	--
1970	18,391	--	--
1972	24,007	14%	--
1974	36,860	19%	19%
1978 Conservative	39,943	10%	2%
1978 High	48,873	13%	7%
Early 1980s			
198? Conservative	53,395	6%	6%
198? Moderate	76,870	12%	16%[a]
198? High	88,875	13%	14%

[a]Calculated from 1978 Conservative.

TABLE III

Forecasts of Population, Families, School Children, Schoolrooms, and Housing Units Needed for
Sweetwater County to the Early 1980s

	Railroad & Construction Families	All Other Basic Families	Local Service Families	Singles (all)	Total Family Population	Total Population	School Children	School-rooms	Incremental Schoolrooms Needed	Incremental Site Homes Needed	Incremental Mobile Home Spaces Needed
1972	990	2,397	2,214	2,190	19,603	21,793	6,721	269	--	--	--
1974	2,730	3,124	2,800	3,771	30,289	34,060	10,385	415	128[a]	1,397	4,599
1978 Conservative	1,170	4,675	3,576	3,393	32,974	36,367	11,305	452	37	2,062	847
1978 High	2,370	4,841	4,240	4,554	40,079	44,633	13,741	550	98	2,398	1,368
1982 Conservative	720	7,310	4,704	4,122	44,569	48,691	15,281	611	61	2,821	1,291
1982 Moderate	2,640	8,968	6,580	6,632	63,658	70,290	21,826	873	262	4,619	5,263
1982 High	3,240	10,710	7,200	7,650	74,026	81,676	25,380	1,015	142	5,627	4,495
Mid-1980s											
Conservative	--	--	--	--	--	--	--	--	--	1,750	--
Moderate	--	--	--	--	--	--	--	--	--	3,294	--
High	--	--	--	--	--	--	--	--	--	4,078	--

[a]Estimated number of District 1 and 2 classrooms in 1974 is 297.

9

2

THE BOOM PROBLEMS

The boom has seriously damaged the quality of life for county residents, the profitability and productivity of industry, and the fiscal viability of local government. Such a wide array of problems assures the interest of many individuals, corporations, and agencies of government in what the problems are and what to do about them.

THE QUALITY OF LIFE HAS BEEN DEGRADED

Sweetwater County is not as pleasant a place to live as it was in 1970. The extremely high growth rate has pushed population beyond the point where existing institutions and ways of doing things are adequate. An examination of housing, health care, education, and other community services provides insight into the quality of life problems in a boom situation.

Housing. The market for permanent housing has broken down and has been unable to provide for the new population. Much of the recently built housing has been at prices which the average trona industry or local service worker cannot afford. Mobile homes have been the only alternative. In 1973, at peak construction, people were living in tents into the month of November because of lack of adequate facilities.

This problem has arisen because:

1. Labor costs are extremely high and labor availability is uncertain. Construction labor for housing must be imported from other labor markets, housed, and guarded against pirating by other employers. One of the largest homebuilders in the Rocky Mountain region recently decided against a 200 unit project in the county for this reason.

2. Both Rock Springs and Green River have little sewage treatment capacity available. This requires developers of large projects to build, in many cases, some treatment facility--an added cost.

3. About half of the land around Rock Springs and Green River is government owned. The remainder, the private land in and around both towns, is closely held by a few owners, with the greatest part owned by Upland Industries, Inc. There is little competition among sellers of land.*

4. As is true throughout the United States, high interest rates have driven home mortgage costs to record highs.

As a result, there are between 4,500 and 5,000 mobile homes in Sweetwater County. Even so, there was an estimated 1974 demand for 1,400 units of permanent housing. It was expected that 800 new units would be completed that year, leaving a deficit of 600 units. It is further estimated that another 2,000 to 2,400 units of permanent housing will be needed by 1978. Also, many of the mobile home residents would prefer permanent housing if it were available.

However, housing prices and home buyers' incomes in Sweetwater County do not match. The average annual income of a miner in Sweetwater County is $11,400 (at $5.50/hour). At two times annual income (the factor used by most mortgage firms to estimate home mortgage borrowing power with present interest rates), the typical mining family with one wage earner could afford to buy, at most, a $25,000 house, or to rent it at $190 to $240 per month. If a second wage earner brings family income up to $17,000 a year, that family could afford up to a $34,000 house.

The average mining family has .3 cats, .9 dogs, 2.0 vehicles, and 2.2 children.† The living space required for this average family tends to be greater than what a mobile home, an apartment, or a small condominium can satisfactorily offer.

Available permanent housing has a hard time fitting these requirements. In one of the largest new developments, Total Concept Development Corporation in 1974 offered single family, detached units of 808 square feet to 1,206 square feet for approximately $33,900 to $43,200, plus a

---

*Upland Industries, Inc. is the real estate subsidiary of Union Pacific Corporation.

†Unpublished trona company survey.

11

homeowners association fee of $414 annually. As an alternative, one trona company is building 1,200 square foot, three bedroom, single family, detached units (without garage) to be rented to its employees for approximately $235 per month.

Health services. In 1970, Sweetwater County had ten doctors, with nine of them engaged in direct delivery of patient care. This was one doctor for every 1,800 people. In July 1974, the county had ten doctors, with eight in direct delivery care (the other two are in radiology and anesthesiology, respectively). Still counting all ten doctors, the ratio is now one to 3,700. The statewide average in Wyoming is one to 1,100.

As a result, health care is a major problem for Sweetwater County residents. It has been estimated that 40 percent of the county's residents obtain medical care elsewhere.* Because of the crowding of the physicians' offices and delays in service, the Rock Springs Hospital emergency room is overburdened with patients, many of them non-emergency cases. It handled an average of 1,300 cases a month during the first quarter of 1974, in spite of the basic charge of $26 for an "office call" at the emergency room.

The mental health clinic caseload at the Southwest Counseling Service in Rock Springs has expanded ninefold in the last five years (while population was not quite doubling). Much of the increase is from long-time residents of the area. Much also is from newcomers; many of these cases are indigent, attracted by the boom but unable to participate in it. As a result, rates of alcoholism, broken homes, suicide and suicide attempts, and down-and-outs have increased.

Fringe development. A substantial share of the population increase since 1970 is housed in mobile home subdivisions or "colonies" sprawled in chaotic fashion throughout the unincorporated areas of the county. An estimated 1,000 mobile homes are presently located in these scattered, isolated fringe developments. These mobile home communities usually lack proper water, sewer, or sanitation facilities. The homes are poorly constructed and create a serious fire hazard.

Such settlements offer little opportunity or encouragement for newcomers to participate in community life.† Social

---

*Sweetwater Health Services, Inc., grant application, April 11, 1974.

†In a recent survey of family attitudes and behavior in another boom community (Gillette, Wyoming), it was

cohesion suffers as alienation and emotional distress feed on each other. Alcoholism, petty crime, educational problems of children, and boredom of spouse are seen in higher proportions among fringe dwellers than among people living in established communities.

Recreation. Recreational, cultural, and adult education facilities have not kept pace with growth. Particularly lacking is organized year-around youth recreation; extensive expansion of indoor facilities is needed. The bowling alleys--often a meeting place for youth--are filled each night with adult leagues. There is no public outdoor swimming pool in the county. The schools hesitate to open their recreation facilities to extra use because they cannot support maintenance crews. A common complaint is lack of enough good restaurants; some older residents, particularly families, hesitate to patronize existing facilities because of crowding and changed atmosphere.

Educational facilities and services.* School facilities are strained beyond capacity in many cases. Both the Rock Springs and Green River school districts have been keeping themselves bonded up to the legal limit (10 percent of assessed valuation, according to the state

---

found that fringe dwellers were less integrated into the community, participated less, and were less satisfied with their situation than people living inside the city limits of a town. This was true even when comparing families of similar income levels and length of residence in the Gillette area. See Doran, Duff, and Gilmore, *Socio-Economic Impacts of Proposed Burlington Northern and Chicago North Western Rail Line in Campbell-Converse Counties, Wyoming* (Denver: Denver Research Institute, 1974). In Sweetwater County, one indicator of integration into the community-- voter registration and voting--strongly suggests that newcomers in general, and fringe newcomers in particular, are not becoming actively involved.

*Although this book deals only with Sweetwater County, the impacts of the boom extend outside it. As more trona-related employees move into Bridger Valley (Uinta County), the school population there increases. From about 360 students in Spring 1973, enrollment grew to 400 in September, 484 in April 1974, and was expected to be 700-800 in September 1974. The school district has no new sources of tax revenue or bonding base.

FMC Corporation, the largest employer of new Bridger Valley residents, has made a $150,000 grant to the school district for a new eight-classroom building. This helps, but the long-term problem is yet to be defined or solved.

13

constitution) and have still been falling behind in needed facilities. After completion of current building programs, using available bonding capacity, the accumulated deficit in facilities needed but not built (e.g., equipment, playgrounds) will add up to an estimated $2 million in the Rock Springs district. The equivalent deficit in Green River district facilities is estimated at over $1 million. And the costs of future growth will probably be substantially more expensive than the growth thus far.

Educational services have also fallen behind those required by growth. Both districts have put financial priority on hiring and retaining teachers and have not been able to budget for needed counseling, school social workers, or other personnel to give needed personal attention to students. Much of the increased enrollment comes from children of semi-transient construction families, many of whom need special help if educational quality is to be maintained for them and for their fellow students. Also, pupil transportation programs have suffered as remote settlements must be serviced by limited numbers of school buses.

   Other problems. The cost of living has risen even faster than the national rate. Housing costs, to buy or rent, have led the increase and housing (as noted earlier) is in very short supply. This is a problem for old-timers (particularly the elderly) and newcomers alike. Salaries, particularly in local services employment, do not appear to have kept up; many residents have suffered from the boom financially, rather than sharing its economic fruits.

Retailing and services facilities have not expanded as rapidly as total employment. Telephone service has suffered. These functions are beginning to catch up, but traffic congestion and parking problems continue to get worse.

Crime rates are up. Complaints to one local law enforcement agency increased 60 percent between 1972 and 1973. Burglary and larceny have increased tremendously. The appearance of street prostitution and drug dealing introduced a new kind of problem for the residents and law enforcement officials of Sweetwater County.

Employment for women has not increased as rapidly as total employment, with its heavy emphasis on construction and mining. Given the problems already mentioned, e.g., inadequate health services, mobile homes in rural isolated developments as the dominant source of new housing, insufficient recreation and leisure time activities, school difficulties, and all the others, *the role of wife and mother is unusually difficult in Sweetwater County.*

14

The quality of life problems are more than mere inconveniences. They are directly damaging to industrial activity in Sweetwater County.

INDUSTRIAL PRODUCTIVITY AND PROFITABILITY HAVE DECLINED

Between Spring 1972 and Spring 1973, tonnage per shift in the trona mines dropped to 60-75 percent of what it was planned to be or what it had been in 1972.

In 1973, employee turnover rose sharply in all of the trona operations. It ranged from 35 percent to 100+ percent in annual rates among the different employers. In December 1973, Stauffer was paying maintenance mechanics and electricians $5.25 per hour; the same men could draw $9.12 per hour and $12 per day subsistence at the Jim Bridger project. Of one trona company's quits in 1973, half were to take other work; most of the others were because new, inexperienced employees could not adapt to mining or to boom conditions in Sweetwater County. In some companies, Canadian workers are being imported in the more skilled crafts because the available labor pool is insufficient.

Construction on the Jim Bridger Power Plant, being built for Pacific Power and Light and Idaho Power by Bechtel Corporation, started in 1971. It was then announced as a $300 million project with a construction force which would peak at 1,200 to 1,500 employees in 1974. The work force reached 3,000 in 1973, and the estimated cost of the project has been scaled up to over $400 million.

All of these problems are primarily attributed to the difficulties of recruiting and retaining satisfactory employees. The regional and even the national labor markets did not function. Assuming the existence of competitive and attractive wages and salaries, much of this difficulty can be attributed to the quality of life problems besetting the community.

THE VIABILITY OF MUNICIPAL GOVERNMENT IS UNCERTAIN

Municipal (and county) employees making $500 to $700 a month in 1973 also were tempted by the industrial and construction wage rates; employee turnover increased. As salaries have been increased in 1974, budgets were strained and needed additional manpower could not be afforded.

The planning function has been sorely neglected in local government (although Rock Springs has done extensive community renewal planning), considering the rates of growth, the magnitude of problems, and the imbalances between

15

resources and needs. (Pitkin County, Colorado, with half the population and half the assessed valuation but with similar growth rates, had a planning staff of six in December 1973; Sweetwater County had a staff of two.)

If urgently needed housing is not provided in Rock Springs and Green River to accommodate present and future growth, the additional demand for municipal services such as police and fire protection and capital construction costs for water, sewer, and sanitation may be beyond their financial capacity.

Even assuming the construction of new homes, the additional assessed valuation from new homes rarely covers the related demands for additional revenues; especially if the new homes are mobile units. And so far, assessed valuation has risen very little with the growth in the two towns, even in inflated current dollars, and not at all in real dollars. Table IV shows how rapidly the real value of the municipal property tax base has declined. Similarly, the real value of the municipal bonds which can be sold (4 percent of assessed valuation, plus 4 percent for sewage disposal system) has declined.

This leaves both municipalities--the necessary cores of urbanization if fringe development is to be avoided--in a very difficult financial situation. They are currently supporting themselves with revenue sharing and a variety of taxes and fees, but these offer no increased borrowing capacity.

TABLE IV

Population and Assessed Valuation

	Population	Current $ Assessed Valuation	Constant $ Valuation (1960 $)	Constant $ Valuation Per Capita
Green River				
1960	3,497	$3.6 million	$3.6 million	$1,029
1970	4,196	5.1	3.9	929
1973	7,000	5.6	3.7	528
Rock Springs				
1960	10,371	$11.9 million	$11.9 million	$1,147
1970	11,657	15.7	12.0	1,029
1973	18,000	16.8	11.1	617

Furthermore, both municipalities are highly dependent on a temporary 1 percent sales tax which must be approved by

16

the voters. Loss of this possibly vulnerable revenue source would be disastrous.

The present municipal revenue and borrowing structure of Rock Springs and Green River (which is largely determined by Wyoming statutes and the Wyoming constitution) does not fit the needs of a boom area like Sweetwater County.

Rock Springs' urban renewal program put a $23 million price tag on refurbishing its neighborhoods, commercial areas, and traffic flows. No similar estimate is yet available for Green River, but it too has a substantial backlog of needed investment. A list of unmet needs, and the costs of meeting some of them, is included in Appendix A.

Government operations in Sweetwater County are also under-financed. They are unable to furnish all of the services and facilities needed by growth thus far, and will have continuing problems with future growth. Because of this, it is difficult to handle many of the quality of life problems already enumerated.

NEW PROBLEMS IN THE FUTURE?

These three categories of problems have resulted from boom rates of growth which have literally outgrown the capacity of such institutions as the housing market, the local labor markets, and the local government financing structure. As the boom growth rate continues, the problems may multiply.

However, the amount of growth is important as well as the rate. A Sweetwater County with a 1984 population of 60,000 to 90,000 will generate some additional problems, even if the current growth rate difficulties are solved.

There will be more intensive pressure on the recreational capability of the area, including the whole outdoors--the hunting and boating and other activities.

Traffic problems in both Green River and Rock Springs may be far worse. Air pollution may become a serious urban problem on still days. The need for public transportation between Rock Springs and Green River will become important.

Labor market problems will probably become worse in the next ten years, if development of domestic fuel sources is pushed by Project Independence. Development of the Powder River Basin coal, the Fort Union lignite deposits, the Four Corners coal deposits, and the Green River oil shale (in Colorado and Utah) will be competing intensively for construction and mining labor. Sweetwater County industrial development will be competing with all of these areas. To compete successfully, it must solve its current and prospective problems.

17

As new population migrates to Sweetwater County, it may bring new life styles and new political orientations. Also, it may create major redistributions of population between Rock Springs, Green River, and some other yet-to-be-identified urban center.

The worst new problem. The worst new problem will be that some additional public facilities will cost more than the community can spend. Yet the existing built-at-low-cost facilities are full, overcrowded; the slack is all used up.

Schools are the prime example, and the easiest to forecast. To take a recent example:

In the last year, population in Sweetwater County increased by an estimated 7,000 people.* Assessed valuation available to school districts increased an estimated $40,000,000, partly from new power plant and chemical plant valuation and partly from increased production of minerals. This is a record increase. Assessed valuation was up $5.7 million per 1,000 new inhabitants, or $570,000 in new school building capacity per 1,000 new inhabitants.

Typically, each 1,000 new inhabitants include 275 school children (the number was probably less than this during the first construction boom, but it will recover or exceed this figure as mining and chemical plant employment becomes more significant). This means that there was about $2,100 in new school bonding capacity per new school child.

Unfortunately, each new school child requires school plant which will cost $5,100, assuming that school constructions costs (including land and equipment) in Sweetwater County are now in the $40-$50 per square foot range.

This suggests a $3,000 per child deficit, given the present constitutional bonding limits, even within a period of substantial growth in assessed valuation.

Further, this suggests that the expected growth in number of children (another 11,441) added to the school load by the early 1980s (moderate forecast) would require $58 million (constant dollars) worth of

*This estimated population increase is based on employment increase in Sweetwater County. The estimate is overstated because some of these people are living in Uinta County. Unless increased population continues to be diverted to neighboring counties, however, the situation described above will exist for years to come.

18

additional schools, *even at present construction costs.*

To finance these within present bonding limits would require $580 million in additional assessed valuation. This means that the assessed value of present mineral production would have to go up sixfold, plus 40 million tons of coal production a year, plus tripled valuation of mining and processing operations, plus power plant valuation at $50 million, all in constant dollars. Given anything like present Wyoming assessment procedures (or those in prospect), this seems unlikely. And if the bonds could be floated, the annual debt service on school bonds would go from $31 per capita in 1973 to $74 per capita in the early 1980s.* This calculation also suggests that even if industry prepaid taxes, the school districts might find it very difficult to *repay* them later.

Yet the schools must be built if the growth occurs. Similar problems will occur in other public facilities furnished by county and municipal governments, but they have more financing flexibility with revenue sharing and/or other governmental capital spending programs.

The identified present and prospective problems must be solved in a difficult and shifting environment.

THE PRESENT ENVIRONMENT FOR PROBLEM SOLVING

These present and prospective problems exist in a political and legislative environment typified by:

1. Local government jurisdictional boundaries which separate sources of public revenues from population centers requiring public services, and which fragment planning efforts. Local rivalries, such as that between Rock Springs and Green River, may aggravate such situations.

2. Limitations on public revenues from *ad valorem* taxes based on limited maximum rates and maximum bond limits based on a low percentage of assessed valuation, rather than on expected (and possibly discounted) public cash flows. Furthermore, Wyoming's philosophy of assessment is against responding rapidly to fast-rising market values.

3. General skepticism about planning at both the local and state levels which delayed inception of community

---

*Assuming 6 percent, 20-year bonds.

development planning, and which apparently still con-
tributes to underestimation of the resources needed
for planning in such a varied and fast-growing community. The planning problems were compounded by the
lack of advance governmental knowledge of industry's
construction and expansion programs.

4. Profound uncertainty and confusion about the roles,
   responsibilities, and future plans of the major corporate interests in Sweetwater County as related to
   growth, community development, and community relations. This, combined with memory of past cutbacks
   in coal mining and rail employment, makes it easy for
   many to assume that much of the present growth is
   temporary and that the problems are equally so.

THE ISSUES RAISED BY BOOM GROWTH

The sampling of problems experienced thus far and forecast
for the future, and the environment in which they must be
solved, suggest the following major issues must be dealt
with:

1. The market does not provide permanent housing in time
   to develop attractive living environments for the in-
   migrants required for mineral development. Similarly,
   public facilities, services, and utilities are not
   provided in timely fashion; the present residents--
   old timers--may be unwilling to vote bonds to benefit
   newcomers perceived as temporary. And even voter
   willingness will not overcome bonding limits set by
   the Wyoming constitution. Conventional evolutionary
   processes of community development and decision
   making do not cope with boom growth. Lead time is
   compressed, future requirements for decisions are not
   recognized in time.

2. Fringe area settlements (most often mobile home communities) develop around existing towns or new centers of employment. These isolated settlements offer
   a substandard quality of life with inadequate urban
   services and little integration into community life.
   They make local government facilities, services, and
   annexation planning more difficult.

3. The area (or multi-state) labor market is no longer
   able to adequately supply skilled or trainable people
   to existing private and public employers. This situation presently exists in underground mining operations in Sweetwater County.

4. Major industrial, community, and personal problems
   result from discontent and depression among wives of

20

in-migrating construction and industrial employees. Neither employment opportunities nor satisfying leisure activities are available for large numbers of women and children.

5. Local governmental jurisdictional boundaries, tax structures, and organizations do not fit the new social and economic community patterns; they are historically developed and generally inflexible to changes in structure.

6. Extensive governmental ownership of land leads to problems of monopoly or oligopoly, and may encourage speculative exploitation of the limited supply of private land.

7. There are few mechanisms for dealing with the urbanization problems of transportation, pollution, and urban sprawl. New settlements--from new towns to trailer or tent colonies--are not adequately regulated or planned for.

8. Institutions or mechanisms do not exist for large firms to cooperate with local government (or among themselves) to solve boom type problems.

9. Future growth in Sweetwater County is related to growing demand for soda ash and energy; should diversification in the local economy be sought to guard against decline, possibly in the next century?

10. Many of these issues are raised not by the magnitude of growth but by *high rates of growth*; it may be necessary to affect rates in order to manage the problems of growth.

The statement of problems and issues contained in Chapter 2 of this book was the authors' first summary of Sweetwater County's boom problems. This statement, along with generalized recommendations for dealing with the problems, was made in a working paper published midway through the research project. These recommendations are reproduced herein as Appendix A - *Concepts and Remedies*.

Completion of the research project focused on problem analysis and further detailing of the initial recommendations. The results were published in January 1975 as a final report and are reproduced in this book as Chapters 3-6.

3
THE PROBLEM TRIANGLE

Sweetwater County has been beset with several boom problems born of very rapid, unmanaged growth in economic activity and population.

Industry representatives in mining and construction, the basic sector of the local economy, agree that productivity and profitability have suffered from the boom.

Local government officials agree that the financial viability of municipalities and schools has been threatened; both capital and operating funds are inadequate. Not only has local government (the public side of the local services sector) suffered, but the private side, including housing and retailing, has also fallen behind booming demand produced by a doubling of population between 1971 and 1974. The entire local service sector is failing to meet community needs for goods and services. In addition, the intangible people-supporting activities have suffered.

Many private citizens agree with industry and governmental officials that the overall quality of life in Sweetwater County has declined during the boom. Newcomers, particularly, are dissatisfied with the community and a majority threaten to leave if housing, health services, and other public and private amenities contributing to quality of life are not promptly improved.*

---

*See *The Residents of Sweetwater County, Wyoming - A Needs Assessment Survey*, hereafter called The Survey, contained as Appendix B of this book. A survey of a cross-section of households in the county was performed by Bickert, Browne, Codding & Associates, Inc. of Denver, under the direction of Carl von E. Bickert, and with supplementary analysis by Mary K. Duff. The survey focused on residents' perception of problems, of priorities for problem solving, and on their housing needs and preferences.

The three categories of boom-town problems--degraded quality of life, declining industrial productivity, and inadequacy of the local service sector--are extremely interdependent. Their relationship to one another is illustrated
below.

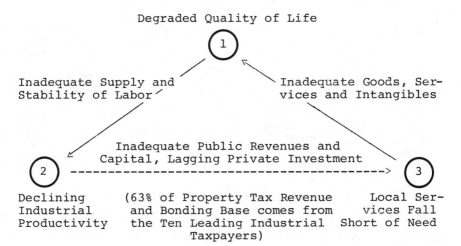

THE PROBLEM TRIANGLE

Degraded Quality of Life

①

Inadequate Supply and
Stability of Labor

Inadequate Goods, Ser-
vices and Intangibles

Inadequate Public Revenues and
Capital, Lagging Private Investment

② ---> ③

Declining   (63% of Property Tax Revenue   Local Ser-
Industrial   and Bonding Base comes from   vices Fall
Productivity   the Ten Leading Industrial   Short of Need
                         Taxpayers)

This self-sustaining cycle will continue unless there is
major change in either the growth that has generated the
problem, or the means of handling growth.

There is a demand for Sweetwater County's natural resources in national (and possibly international) markets.
(See Table I, page 4.) The prime limitation on growth of
economic activity is the community's ability to accommodate more people.

Though growth is unlikely to stop, rates of growth may
vary. Population growth has now slowed somewhat from the
1971-1973 compounded annual rate of about 20 percent.
Substantial layoffs of largely transient construction
workers will come as individual projects approach completion. But as Table I illustrated, new construction will
be initiated and growth will continue. If growth *rates*
in employment slump in the mid-1970s, they will probably
rise again in the late 1970s. And even if the *rates* of
growth decline, total employment is expected to continue
its increase.

The type of growth may also change, as emphasis shifts
from construction to permanent mining and processing operations, and as the local service sector employment catches
up to demand.

If growth can be handled, the population (and the outputs
of the county) will continue to rise at least into the
early 1980s. (See Figure 1, page 7.)

CHANGING THE MEANS OF HANDLING GROWTH

If growth is to be well managed, the problem triangle must
be broken. Substantial progress has already been made.
Rock Springs and the county have obtained state assistance
to solve the immediate problem of financing hospital construction. School bonds are still passing, up to existing
bonding limits, across the county. Plans are being made
for a sewage disposal plant. Green River has bonded itself for public facilities. Land use planning, zoning,
and zoning enforcement are all underway. Industry has
contributed financial and other aid on a variety of problems. A committee of the Wyoming State Legislature has
studied and recommended several new methods of problem
solving.

Probably the most hopeful note is the establishment of the
Sweetwater County Priorities Board, and its counterpart
industry association.* This local effort at developing
new institutional methods of handling growth has received
the support of state government and industry, and has the
potential to mobilize and coordinate far more resources
than have yet been available. The Board can also help to
apply and distribute the resources.

Most of what has been accomplished so far, however, has
been in reaction to growth crises. The boom-type growth
process itself is not self-managing or self-moderating.

---

*The Sweetwater County Priorities Board was proposed
in July 1974 and established that November, as was the
Southwest Wyoming Industrial Association. The Board has
eight elected officials (county commissioners and mayors),
five industry representatives selected by the Association,
and two citizens at large plus a citizen advisory group.
In early 1975, the Board set health services priorities
ahead of educational buildings; in May 1975 the Association responded with $200,000 in grants and loan guarantees
for clinic expansion and administration. Both groups were
cooperating in obtaining National Health Service Corps and
individual physicians for the region.

24

Several questions must be answered before plans can be made for breaking the problem triangle.

1. What is the community economic growth process and how does it work?

2. What happened to this process during the Sweetwater County boom? Why did the problem triangle develop?

3. Can boom-type growth be managed to improve the community *and* to make higher growth rates tolerable?

4. What tools can be used for effective growth management?

5. What are the roles of the Priorities Board, local government, industry, and the public in growth management?

The remaining chapters will deal with these questions.

4

THE GROWTH PROCESSES

The Sweetwater County boom is a case in which the traditional processes regulating economic growth have not
worked well. The market mechanisms which are supposed to
furnish the factors of production and smooth growth or
decline in production have not done so.*

THE MARKET MECHANISMS

When major new capital investments were made in Sweetwater
County (for production of soda ash, electricity, coal), according to conventional economic wisdom, the markets for
the other factors of production should have responded.
The labor market would supply the needed employees. The
land and materials markets would be able to meet demands
made on them. The capital market would permit the financing of housing for the new employees and their families, and of facilities to supply goods and services such
as education, streets and highways, and health care.

This increased demand for these factors might push local
prices up a little (including wages, the price of labor),
but presumably the required factors would be available.

---

*According to classical economic theory, the factors
of production are land, labor, and capital. A market exists for each factor, and determines the supply and price
of each factor. Land (M) includes land and materials, and
in this case, combinations of these into productive plant.
Labor (L) includes all those who gather, combine, or con-
vert M. Capital (I) is the investment capital required to
obtain M and L from their respective markets and to as-
semble them into product (P), which is then sold to maintain the process. Thus, production is a function of the
amounts and proportions of the factors, or $P=f(M,L,I)$.

The growth processes would work satisfactorily, controlled and assisted by the markets for the factors of production.

The situation before major new capital investment and the idealized situation *after* plant construction are shown in Figures 2 and 3, respectively.

THE STABLE SITUATION

A stable or slowly growing community is depicted in Figure 2.

The factors of production in the basic sector. Basic capital (I_b) has been invested in land and materials assembled into an existing stock of productive plant and facilities (M_b), and in working capital to keep material inputs flowing through the plant. This employs basic labor (L_b).

The local economy's basic or export sector produces goods and services which are sold elsewhere, e.g., to national markets. In return for those exports, basic income and purchasing power is *imported* and is distributed locally through wage payments and purchases.* This purchasing power supports the local service sector, until it "leaks" back out of the local economy as retailers restock their shelves, and money is spent elsewhere.

The factors of production in the local service sector. Similarly, local service capital (I_s) has been invested, resulting in both public and private facilities (M_s) producing goods and services for the local population. This employs local service labor (L_s).

Local service activities include those provided by local government, e.g., education, streets and highways, public safety, welfare, mental health, and usually sewer and water service. Many other local service activities are provided by private businesses, e.g., retailing, personal services, energy and telecommunications, and construction --including housing. Health services are provided by private physicians and other practitioners and public hospitals. Other social support services are furnished less formally by churches, voluntary associations, clubs, and friendly people.

---

*In a small community with a wealthy population, e.g., Aspen, Colorado, income from property or investments elsewhere is also a source of basic purchasing power. In a suburban community, much of the basic income may come from those commuting to jobs in the central city.

FIGURE 2

COMMUNITY GROWTH MODEL: THE STABLE SITUATION

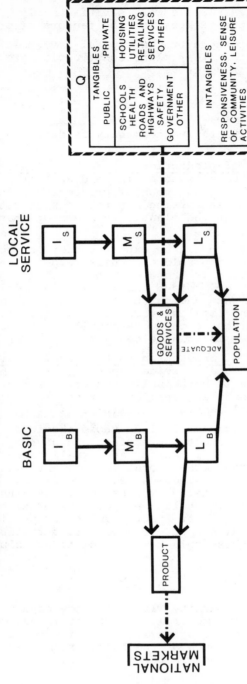

P = f(M,I,L)
I - INVESTMENT CAPITAL
M - LAND & MATERIALS
     (SOMETIMES CONVERTED INTO PLANT)
L - LABOR
Q - QUALITY OF LIFE

━━━━ MAKES POSSIBLE, SUPPORTS, USES
━·━·━ MARKET DEMAND, REQUIREMENT
■■■■ IS EQUAL TO

28

Labor and population. Except for commuters, labor (both L_b and L_s) is drawn from the local population. The laborers--in all occupations--support the households that make up the local population. The continuing availability of L_b and L_s depends on a sufficiently large and stable local population. Thus, the local population and the labor force are mutually dependent.

Basic to local service relationships. In the stable or moderate growth situation (up to 5 percent annual growth rate), the local services are generally those desired and affordable by the local population. Capital to furnish new local service facilities (including housing) is usually available from various investors, barring national upsets in capital markets.

For each employee in basic industry, there are usually from one to two local service employees in a typical, stable, small Rocky Mountain community, so the basic-to-local-service multiplier is from 1 to 2. And in a stable or slowly growing community, the local services sector can be expected to grow (both L_s and I_s) in appropriate proportion to growth in basic L and I. A sudden change in this multiplier is apt to signal a change in the quantity of goods and services available to the population, and thus in the material aspects of the quality of life, Q.

The quality of life. The quality of life, Q, of the entire population depends on two things: 1) tangible aspects, e.g., the adequacy of the goods and services available and affordable in the local service sector; and 2) intangible aspects, e.g., the morale and attitudes of the population in relation to such things as adequate leisure activities, responsive government, and a supportive spirit of community.

THE EFFECTS OF MAJOR INCREASES IN BASIC PLANT INVESTMENT

To start a growth situation, corporate or governmental decisions are made in favor of new or incremental major capital investments, ΔI_b. These are used to construct and operate new basic plants, ΔM_b. This represents a large increment or addition to the stock of basic capital in the local community. It will also require additional employees, ΔL_b, for both construction and operation. These increments Δ are shown added to the existing basic sector in Figure 3.

The additional employment will create increased population (Δ population). The increase in construction employment (and related population) may be very fast, and much of the labor for it will probably come in from outside the community. Some people may be hired away from jobs already in the community, interfering with the existing balance

29

FIGURE 3

COMMUNITY GROWTH MODEL: INCREMENTAL CHANGE, BALANCED GROWTH.

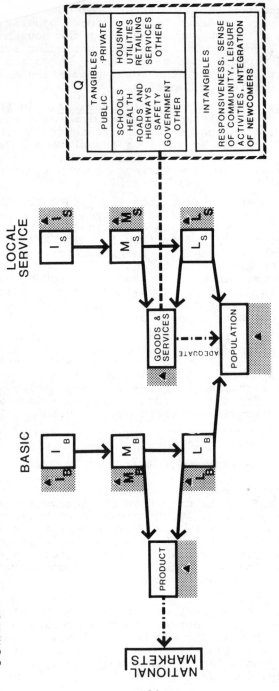

P = f(M,I,L)
I - INVESTMENT CAPITAL
M - LAND & MATERIALS
    (SOMETIMES CONVERTED INTO PLANT)
L - LABOR
Q - QUALITY OF LIFE
◄ - INCREMENT

——— MAKES POSSIBLE, SUPPORTS, USES
–·–·– MARKET DEMAND, REQUIREMENT
– – – IS EQUAL TO

between basic and local service activities.

In any case, the new basic sector population must be accommodated, and the local service sector must expand to do this. Additional local service capital investment, ΔI_s, is induced (or required by the new basic investment.* Local service employment, ΔL_s, also must be expanded to maintain levels of service. These increments are shown added to the local service sector in Figure 3.

   The ideal case--balanced growth. Even in a small community, large increments to population can be accommodated, *if* the additional local service capital, ΔI_s, is invested in timely fashion. Not only must adequate ΔI_s, ΔM_s, and ΔL_s be combined to produce additional local service goods and services, but all of the intangibles mentioned, plus one more, must be assured to maintain Q, the quality of life. The additional intangible is integration: new population must be integrated into the established community as they arrive and as they desire.

If the population attracted by the new jobs resulting from ΔI_b (and from ΔI_s) can be accommodated while maintaining

---

*The induced local service capital investment (ΔI_s) required to maintain quality of life apparently may be from 5 percent to 20 percent of the new basic investment (ΔI_b), depending on the type of plant being built.
   Accommodating the construction force and related population on a power plant where ΔI_b is $500 million may require ΔI_s of $30-50 million, depending on housing arrangements. The ΔI_s requirements for the permanent operation (including local coal mining) is apt to require $20 million more. Up to half of the ΔI_s is in the public facilities.
   The ΔI_s requirement to balance a ΔI_b of $800 million in a more labor intensive coal gasification plant will be from $80-140 million during the construction phase. The ΔI_s requirement for permanent operation will run $70-90 million. (All of these very rough estimates are in 1974 dollars.)
   The contrast between ΔI_s requirements for the construction phase and for the operating phase raises questions about the desirability of dispersing plant construction among different communities, each of which then has to go through the same cycle of expansion and contraction. An argument can be made for concentrating such industrial activities in one geographic area and phasing construction to avoid sharp peaks and valleys.

the quality of life, adequate labor will be available.
Additional product can be produced and exported as
planned, and this should lead to adequate returns on the
additional basic investment, ΔI_b.

Even in this ideal case, there may be a problem getting
adequate returns on the new local service investment, ΔI_s,
if it was built up to accommodate a one-time construction
increment with an ensuing drop off. This raises the issue
of who should pay for such investment, the employers of
the construction force, the public, in the form of the
permanently existing tax base, or some combination of the
two.

   Unbalanced growth. Major new basic investment, ΔI_b,
which is *not* balanced by adequate and timely local service
investment, ΔI_s, is inevitably upsetting.

If the local service sector cannot adequately expand its
facilities, employment, and output of goods and services
to meet increased demand, there is less for everyone.
This in itself degrades the material quality of life Q,
even as prices and rents are being driven up. Further, if
the intangibles of quality of life also are less satisfactory, both the established and the new population suffer.
This situation is depicted in Figure 4.

As quality of life declines, people are more apt to leave.
The labor supply shrinks, relative to demand. If the labor supply cannot meet labor demand, productivity suffers
in both basic and local service sectors.

This describes briefly what happened during the Sweetwater
County boom: the markets for the factors of production
did not function to make growth proceed smoothly. The
Problem Triangle described earlier was created and continues into 1975.

Information was lacking for timely and adequate local service investment, ΔI_l. Had the information been available,
the investment might or might not have been sought, and
the capital markets might or might not have supplied the
money. Timely investment was not made, and local service
goods and services, both public and private, fell behind.
As private services lagged behind demand, more was asked
of the public sector, both local and state government.
But its resources are restricted by rigorous limitations
on bonding capacity and on flexibility in taxation. Furthermore, if the boom is perceived as temporary, with a
decline to follow, voters are hesitant to vote for bonds.

The new population was not adequately provided with either
the tangibles or the intangibles of quality of life Q.
The additional population was not adequately housed and
integrated into established communities, so the labor market did not function well. Employee turnover increased,

FIGURE 4

COMMUNITY GROWTH MODEL: UNBALANCED GROWTH

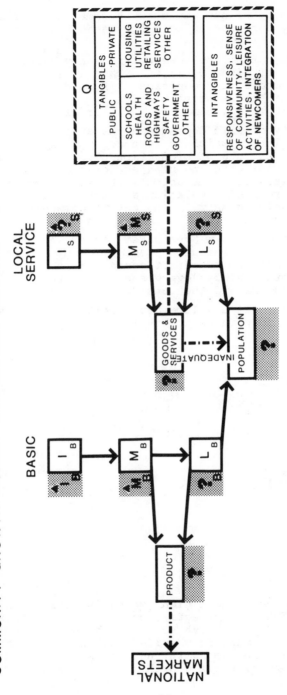

P = f(M,I,L)

I - INVESTMENT CAPITAL

M - LAND & MATERIALS
    (SOMETIMES CONVERTED INTO PLANT)

L - LABOR

Q - QUALITY OF LIFE

▲ - INCREMENT

——— MAKES POSSIBLE, SUPPORTS, USES

—·—·— MARKET DEMAND, REQUIREMENT

— — — IS EQUAL TO

and recruitment of new employees became more difficult. Productivity suffered in both the basic and local service sectors.*

One conclusion from the Sweetwater County experience is that quality of life, Q, in this case is as important as the three factors of production M, L, and I. In a remote community which must attract and retain labor from elsewhere, quality of life may *be* a factor of production.

Since quality of life depends on the availability of local service labor (which in turn depends on the availability of other factors of production plus the intangibles), L_S must be considered and planned for along with L_b. It is as necessary to satisfactorily house and serve the local service related population as that population supported by basic industry. The entire community must be developed, not just the industrial segment.

Finally, the growth in Sweetwater County was not mismanaged so much as it was unmanaged. The adjustments to growth were left up to market mechanisms that did not or could not work. Almost every segment of the local community suffered, as did the outside investors in ΔI_b.

The alternative is a deliberate effort at growth management by all the parties-at-interest to growth.

---

*The Survey showed high job satisfaction (including income and future prospects), but extreme dissatisfaction with such items as health services, housing, and recreation, prompting many to consider leaving the community. This was most true among the newcomers who must be attracted and retained if growth is to continue.

5

BOOM TOWN GROWTH MANAGEMENT

Growth management, as it is used here, does not mean centralized control of economic activity and growth by a government agency or an industrial firm or group. Growth management does involve generating enough cooperation among the groups and persons involved to develop the economic, political, and social tools needed, and to use them to implement consensus solutions to the following questions.

1. Where should new employment and new population be located?

2. What should the rate of growth be?

3. How should the benefits of growth be shared?

4. How should the costs of growth be paid for, and who should pay for them?

5. How can the parties-at-interest to growth* be brought together to *manage* growth?

The answers to these questions, if they represent a consensus, can be expressed as sets of objectives, some of which are specific enough to allow measuring performance. Examples of such hierarchies of objectives are given in the following chapter.

---

*The parties-at-interest to community growth management include industry, state, local and federal government, commercial interests, the public, etc.

The limit of the community growth process is not known, but in the unmanaged growth situation described earlier an annual population growth rate of 10 percent strains local service capabilities. A rate of 15-20 percent seems to cause breakdowns in local and regional institutions, such as the housing market and the labor market. The quality of life then declines, and this affects industrial operations which depend on a stable and satisfied work force.

Good growth management could help avoid seemingly intolerable rates of growth. It might also raise the ceiling of what growth rates are tolerable,* if the costs and intangible needs arising from growth were met.

Given the existence of this uncertainty about the limits of growth, the essential functions of growth management appear to be: 1) balancing basic and induced capital investment; 2) affecting resource use and conservation; 3) developing labor force; and 4) accommodating and retaining population. The applicability of these functions (and the need for all of them) is diagrammed in Figure 5.

FUNCTION 1: BALANCING BASIC AND INDUCED CAPITAL INVESTMENT

Induced capital investment, ΔI_s, in local service facilities, including housing, sewer, and schools, must be adequate both in dollar amount and timing to accommodate increased population resulting from the incremental investment in basic plant, ΔI_b. One way to balance the two types of investment is to augment the availability of induced, local service investment capital. Another is to limit the magnitude or rate of basic capital investment.

Either way, *balancing* requires open communication between investment decision makers in the basic sector and those in the local service sector. The Sweetwater County Priorities Board is an innovative approach to such communication. It provides a forum for monthly meetings between elected officials, basic industry representatives, and citizens (representing the local service sector). This procedure requires an industry organization (The Southwest Wyoming Industrial Association) and staff for the Priorities Board.

Time lags between identifying the induced capital need,

---

*Calculating and estimating this limit, under conditions of good growth management, is beyond the scope of this project.

FIGURE 5

COMMUNITY GROWTH MODEL: GROWTH MANAGEMENT FUNCTIONS

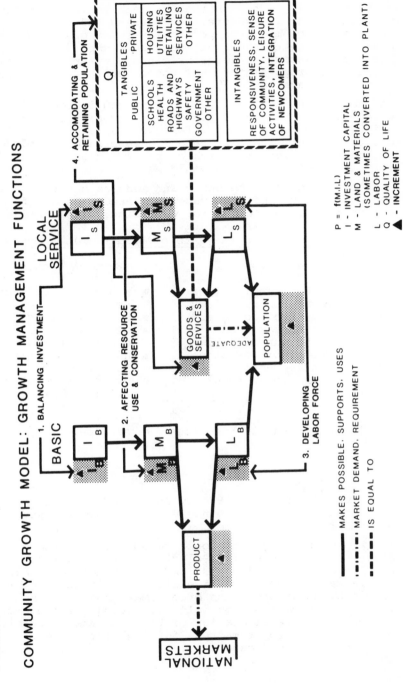

P = f(M,I,L)
I - INVESTMENT CAPITAL
M - LAND & MATERIALS
    (SOMETIMES CONVERTED INTO PLANT)
L - LABOR
Q - QUALITY OF LIFE
▲ - INCREMENT

━━━ MAKES POSSIBLE, SUPPORTS, USES
━·━·━ MARKET DEMAND, REQUIREMENT
━━ ━━ IS EQUAL TO

ΔI_S, and having money in the bank are serious problems in financing schools, sewers, and housing--12 to 36-month periods are common. Corporate investors must give maximum advance notice to the local service sector. They may even find it necessary to defer or cancel investment if it appears that proportionate balancing local service investment is not available.*

The ratios between basic investment and induced investment will probably vary substantially. A coal gasification plant will be more labor intensive than a coal-fired steam electric plant; it will therefore require more induced investment. Further research on these ratios and the factors that influence them would be very useful.

Ways of affecting both basic and induced capital investment so they may be reasonably balanced, and of affecting the communication needed for balancing, are listed below.

Means of Affecting the Rate of Basic Capital Investment†

Deterrents	Encouragements
■ plant site planning laws ■ plant site control laws ■ industry-specific taxes[a] ■ policies or taxes encouraging out-of-region processing of resources ■ impact statements ■ permit or impact fees[a] ■ zoning	■ industrial development bonds ■ loan guarantees ■ industry-specific accelerating depreciation ■ industry-specific income tax credits ■ government construction of plants or facilities

[a]Passed in the 1975 legislative session.

*The decision in 1974 by Idaho Power not to build an additional Sweetwater County electric power plant, fueled by coal from Black Buttes, is an example of this.

†Growth management tools recommended to the Wyoming State Legislature by its Select Committee on Industrial Development Impact (the Ostlund Committee), December 1974. The package is an impressive effort to identify growth problems, determine means or estimate costs for solving them, and recommend remedial legislation. The estimates of costs and the allocation of taxes to the beneficiaries of growth are proper matters for legislative review, but the approach seems exemplary.

Means of Affecting the Rate of Induced Capital (Local
Service) Investment

Deterrents	Encouragements
■ low bonding limits ■ low assessment ratios ■ high land prices ■ lack of state or federal financial aid	■ public facility grants ■ public facility loans[a] ■ exemptions or increased bonding limits[a] ■ "pay-as-you-grow" tap fees and permit fees ■ state development authority (i.e., Wyoming Community Development Authority)[a] ■ company assured housing ■ joint powers (multi-government cooperation) legislation[a] ■ local flexibility in taxations, including income taxes ■ industry loans to local service entities ■ industrial development bonds for local service activities, including retailing ■ state revenue sharing[a] ■ impact fees[a]* ■ low interest housing purchase loans[a]

[a]Passed in the 1975 legislative session.

Means of Affecting Communication Among Sectors

Deterrents	Encouragements
■ traditional industry views that most information is proprietary ■ closed or nonparticipative local government budgeting	■ joint industry-government problem-solving (the Sweetwater County Priorities Board) ■ industry and citizen participation in local

*Fees charged to new industry by local government to
cover ΔI_s costs, and required by statute or by contract as
condition for rezoning or construction permit, as done by
Skagit County, Washington, and Puget Sound Power and Light
Company.

- inadequate local gov-
  ernment planning
- uncertainty about fed-
  eral land and resource
  policies
- inadequate coordination
  and cooperation among
  units of government

- government budget
  preparation
- joint industry-govern-
  ment local planning
  staff
- voluntary industry dis-
  closure of tentative
  investment and site
  planning
- legislation requiring
  environmental impact
  and community impact
  statements
- industrial site control
  legislation requiring
  information
- industrial site control
  legislation requriing
  justification
- aggressive press cover-
  age of local economic
  and political activities

FUNCTION 2:   AFFECTING RESOURCE USE AND CONSERVATION

Land use has been regulated to some extent by state governments for 50 years, water use for even longer. Both
affect the specific location of various economic activities. State regulation to maintain air quality and water
quality has more recently been mandated by federal legislation. States are increasingly legislating controls on
mining and land reclamation practices. Traditional state-
fixed mineral production quotas (ostensibly for resource
conservation but also related to price maintenance) are
currently out of favor. Minerals taxation affects the
economics (and thus the extent) of minerals recovery.

Some of the tools that can be used to affect resource use
are listed below.

Means of Affecting Resource Use

Deterrents

- exclusionary zoning
- preservation of agricul-
  tural or other existing
  uses by zoning or tax
- emission and effluent
  regulations

Encouragements

- permissive zoning
- release of public lands
- easing the transfer of
  water rights and the
  acquisition of uncom-
  mitted water

40

- complex source and non-degradation regulations for air quality
- siting controls
- use quotas (grazing or logging public lands)

- "industrial development" standards of air quality*
- differential tax rates, favoring production of certain minerals or qualities of minerals
- control of annexations, municipal incorporations and formation of special districts

FUNCTION 3:   DEVELOPING LABOR FORCE

Balancing of labor supply and labor demand is as important as balancing basic and induced capital investment. Both functions are difficult during periods of rapid growth. The labor supply in a boom community generally depends on the community's ability to attract labor and accompanying households from other, competing labor markets. Secondarily, labor supply depends on the ability of local industry and government to increase the labor participation rate to attract, train, and retain a greater proportion of those persons already living in the area.

On the demand side, balance may be achieved by minimizing labor requirements. More off-site construction work may be done outside the region, both in basic plant construction (e.g., electrical and piping subsystems) and in local service construction (e.g., manufactured modules for buildings and housing).

Some of the tools to be used for developing labor force are listed below.

Increase the Supply and Utilization of Labor

Deterrents

- limit local service investment so that community is relatively unattractive
- fail to maintain intangibles of the quality of life

Encouragements

- develop and maintain attraction capability, e.g., good wages and career opportunities, quality of life sufficient to increase population and labor force

---

*Air quality maintenance regions must be set up by the states, according to the Clean Air Act of 1970 as interpreted by the courts. An "industrial development" region would presumably have the lowest air quality standard permissible.

41

- comparatively lower wage scales for local government employees than for mining, construction

- establish training programs
- encourage local affirmative action activity
- maintain day care centers to encourage women to participate
- offer relocation allowances
- award longevity job seniority bonuses
- offer competitive job security or income security

Affect the Demand for Labor

Deterrents

- encourage off-site construction to be done outside area
- discourage processing or conversion of extracted minerals
- limit expansion of local service employment by discouraging induced capital investment

Encouragements

- encourage local mineral processing and conversion
- encourage induced capital investment (ΔI_s)

FUNCTION 4:   ACCOMMODATING AND RETAINING POPULATION

Growth in economic activity generally requires more labor. If the growth is to be lasting (and profitable), a substantial part of the labor force must be willing to settle in the community. In most cases (certainly in the Rocky Mountain Region), this requires accommodation of the additional employees' families.

Successful accommodation of new families requires adequate local services and amenities,* comparable to those the same families could find in other communities with comparable employment opportunities. Many of these local services and amenities depend on adequate induced local service capital investment, ΔI_s. Some depend on the

---

*The provision of adequate local services and amenities also requires additional local service employees as mentioned previously, whose families must be accommodated as well. It is not sufficient merely to attract and retain basic (construction and mining) employees and their families.

friendliness of long-time residents and the willingness of newcomers to participate in community life.

Examples of such tools are given below.

Accommodating and Retaining Population

Deterrents	Encouragements
■ failure to encourage (opposite column) and failure to manage growth during boom are major deterrents	■ adequate wages and career opportunities ■ housing at affordable prices, lease-purchase agreements with employer financing ■ health services ■ adequate education, recreation, leisure time activities ■ safety and security ■ newcomer integration into the community ■ land continuingly available for housing to avoid monopolistic pricing ■ easy access to participation in community affairs

6

A HIERARCHY OF
OBJECTIVES LEADING TO
PROGRAM PACKAGES AND
A DECISION AGENDA

Boom problems exist in Sweetwater County because the institutions traditionally expected to regulate growth have not done so. On the other hand, the four functions of growth management are known and many tools to carry them out are identifiable. If growth is to be managed to achieve what the community--including industry--wants, the community's objectives must be defined.

OBJECTIVES

Objectives may be expressed as abstract good intentions, but they become useful only as they are more specifically stated. To be operationally useful, they must describe, often quantitatively, a situation which solves (or is solving) a problem or which achieves (or is achieving) an opportunity.

An objective may reflect a time deadline or may acknowledge limitations imposed by conflicting policies and goals of the institutions and groups involved. A usable operational objective statement must make it possible to tell whether or not the objective is being achieved. The operational objective should also be clearly related to broader goals.

Objectives are not isolated. Objectives are most easily achieved when they are part of a broader structure, or hierarchy, which knits them together. Such a hierarchy is presented later in this chapter with hypothetical examples of objectives for Sweetwater County. The actual objectives must be developed by community consensus with broad participation by all parties at interest to growth.

Sweetwater County has a good forum for developing consensus objectives in the Priorities Board. With strong citizen participation the Board should be able to establish a

44

hierarchy of objectives and guide implementation programs for achieving them.

A broad consensus is vital. Consensus objectives, and the consensus-making process, are an important supplement to the limited police power and budget power of local government. The more who participate in the consensus, the more who are educated and influenced by it.

The conventional settings for community planning are committees, hearings, and interest group meetings. To these can be added neighborhood caucuses, mass media capabilities, and polling and feedback techniques. An ideal public consensus would be: democratic, restorative of social cohesion, moderating of extreme positions, and a vital input to growth planning and management, influencing public and private decisions.

Decision making by consensus encourages voluntary, cooperative growth management, rather than unilateral use of police power or economic power. The roles of the parties-at-interest in various growth management activities are outlined in Table V.

THE HIERARCHY

An example of an ordered set of objectives is presented below:

Growth management policy. A grand goal, a statement of good intentions.

To "achieve a balance between population and resource use which will permit high standards of living and a wide sharing of life's amenities."*

Threat. General statement of the problem, of the activities generating a potential threat to the grand goal.

Between 1970 and 1974 Sweetwater County has been growing at a 19 percent annual rate, more than doubling its population. Industrial investment in expansion of existing plant or creation of new plant has been the primary cause of this growth. The rate and magnitude has created a disruptive boom situation in the community. Given the national energy crisis and growing international markets for natural soda ash, resource development in Sweetwater County will provide the

*National Environmental Policy Act, Sec. 101(b)(5).

TABLE V

Roles in Growth Management Activities

	Growth Management Policy	Threat	Threat Response Policy	Operational Threat	Operational Objectives	Operational Threat Responses Policies	Detailed Operational Objectives	Program Packages	Agenda
Public (through advisory groups, volunteer associations, etc.)	Suggest	Review	Suggest and review	Review	Review, modify, and support	Review and approve	Review and approve	Help implement, evaluate	Review
Priorities Board and staff	Collect consensus	Research, forecast, and define	Collect consensus	Define	Propose	Propose	Propose	Prepare, coordinate, and evaluate	Prepare annually, suggest revisions
Local government; legislation or decisions	Suggest and review	Review	Suggest and review	Review	Review, modify, and adopt	Review and approve	Review and approve	Implement	Review
State government; legislation or decisions	Observe	Observe	Observe	Observe	Observe and advise	Observe and advise	Observe, advise, and assist	Assist in implementation and finance	Review

basis for continued rapid growth for at least another 20 years (with a projected range of between 53,000-89,000 people by the early 1980s).

Threat Response Policies. General policy statement responding to specifically described threat, or otherwise authorizing response.

To maintain a viable community, better accommodating population and thus improving productivity in a competitive regional market; to see that the social and public costs of growth are borne equitably and that inequitably borne growth costs not be incurred.

Operational Threats. Actual or potential problem, more precisely defined, for which remedial policies are being sought.

The local services sector of Sweetwater County lags far behind the demand for services. The fiscal viability of local government is threatened. These then become primary factors in the degradation of quality of life experienced by residents since 1971. This is evidenced by the collapse of the housing and health services market, by increased crime, divorce, and alcoholism rates, and by overcrowded schools and overburdened sewer systems. The failure to maintain community "liveability" has led to reduced industrial productivity and thus profitability as workers are dissatisfied and often leave the area. Increased competition with other resource development regions (e.g., Powder River, North Dakota) for employees and population will further threaten Sweetwater County's ability to attract an adequate labor force.

Operational Objectives. Indicator of desired achievement, written to describe a situation in which the threat exists at or below an acceptable level.

To stabilize the county growth rate at between 7 and 10 percent annually, or at the highest rate tolerable under good growth management, to stimulate expansion of both public and private local service so that within three years the basic to local service multiplier equals

47

1.6, the pre-boom relationship.
To return to 1971 levels of
productivity for trona and coal
mined per unit per shift.   To
achieve by 1979 slack capacity
in public facilities (particularly water and sewer) that
will accommodate an immediate
incremental population of
15,000 and commensurate capability for rapidly adding 100
classrooms.

To restore the quality of life
to a desirable level of "liveability."   An attitudinal survey (similar to that in Appendix B of this book) taken in
1977 should indicate that 1)
only 5-7 percent of respondents
would expect to leave the area
despite a stable employment
situation; 2) that 80-90 percent would consider the community improving or positively
stabilized; 3) that 65 percent
would desire to remain in the
area for the rest of their
lives, and achieve 80-90 percent willingness to stay in the
community by 1979; and 4) given
a list of services to compare
with former places of residence,
Sweetwater County should be
ranked equal or above satisfaction on at least half.

Operational Threat
Response Policy Categories.
Categories of remedial policies in response to op-
erational threat and operational objectives.
    Such policies are
guides to choosing and
defining detailed opera-
tional objectives.   They
would also affect current
decision-making (see
agenda examples for 1976
and 1978).

1.   Increase the comparative
advantage of Sweetwater County
as an enjoyable place for the
individual and family to live
and work, and as a profitable
area in which to do business.

2.   Assure governmental institutional capabilities (including fiscal and capital
structure viability) to accommodate growth.

3.   Encourage a public-private
partnership approach to managing growth which involves
maximum citizen participation.

4. Distribute the public and social costs of growth equally among the beneficiaries of that growth.

Detailed Operational Objectives. Indicators of desired achievement written to describe a situation in which the threat exists at or below an acceptable level.

Described below.

Program Packages. Sets of program components (projects and implementation tools) which together will achieve the detailed operational objective.

Described below.

Detailed operational objectives (DOOs) may be numerous and will necessarily address a variety of problem areas. It is important that they be determined by community consensus. A setting using broad citizen participation helps generate solutions and sometimes alternatives (program packages) for achieving the objectives, and often indicates priorities for action.

The following list of detailed operational objectives presents some hypothetical examples for purposes of demonstration. The objectives are based on interviews and The Survey, and reflect what *might* result from an actual objective setting process by Sweetwater County citizen representatives, elected officials, and industry spokesmen.

The detailed operational objectives are interdependent, just as the problems they deal with are interdependent. See the Problem Triangle in Chapter 3. They must all fit together within the hierarchy of goals and objectives, and they must *all* be achieved if the goals, objectives, and policies are to be met.

DETAILED OPERATIONAL OBJECTIVES

1. Plans should be made for completion of the new Sweetwater County Hospital on schedule, and adequate clinical facilities, physicians, and other staff to provide quality health services within maximum time limits and within agreed upon cost limits with fixed milestones of progress showing partial accomplishment by September 1975. (An actual detailed operational objective should be prepared under the direction of the Priorities Board by March 1975. The

information and expertise available through Sweetwater Health Services, Inc., should be particularly helpful. Such an objective might include recruiting specialists, providing housing for medical staff, creating a drug counseling and treatment service through Sweetwater Counseling Service, and establishing outpatient clinics in Reliance and/or Superior.)

2. The Sweetwater County Priorities Board should be the catalyst for an undertaking that will produce up to 4,000 units of detached single family unit housing constructed and available between now and the end of 1977,* of a quality augmenting the quality of life. If Jim Bridger Power Plant unit #5 construction is not underway, at least 2,000 such units should be made available by the end of 1977. Sixty percent of these houses should be available for sale with monthly payments not exceeding 20 percent of the average trona miner's income (estimated at $1,125 a month), or $225 per month in 1974 dollars. Another 20 percent (not necessarily detached single units) should be available to those employed in the local service sector with rental or purchase payments of $175 per month.

3. Additional grade separations (between streets and rail tracks) are needed at both Green River and Rock Springs on the Union Pacific main line. One additional separation is needed for each city by the end of 1976. A grade separation over the Union Pacific northbound line from Rock Springs will be needed at Grant Street by the time two or more unit trains of coal are running daily.

4. Wastewater treatment facilities now under study for Green River and Rock Springs should be completed by 1977, with continuing planning for satellite facilities in rural areas and for growth in the larger settlements.

5. A joint county-towns sanitary landfill operation

---

*This figure is derived from Table III, page 9, and was determined by adding the 1974 housing deficit plus 75 percent of "mobile home spaces needed," plus 100 percent of "incremental site homes needed." The necessity to include 75 percent of mobile homes here as permanent homes reflects information from The Survey (Appendix B). Survey results indicate a substantially higher proportion of individuals desire permanent homes than had been assumed by the authors in calculating Table III prior to administering The Survey.

should be equipped and working by 1976.

6. An enlarged County Services staff with a nucleus of present professionals, but expanded to include sanitation workers, building inspectors, and specialists in planning, budgeting, public administration, grant application, and engineering (some loaned personnel from industry may be included) should be available to all local government agencies. A committee of town and county staff should prepare a list of needs, and ways of sharing personnel.

7. The costs, revenues, and capital improvements plans for all major units of government should be on a five-year planning basis by 1976. By 1979, all major units of government should have adequate sources of revenue and capital under Wyoming statutes and constitutional provisions then in existence to accommodate steady growth. Tax incidence should be designed so that the net costs of growth are borne by the beneficiaries of growth.

8. Construction and availability of several small community centers should be underway by fall of 1977. These would be used for adult and youth activities and offer any or all of the following: movie theater, bowling lanes, pool hall, indoor and outdoor swimming pools, skating rink, tennis courts, meeting rooms. Some of these facilities should be built and owned by private enterprise and might be housed under one roof.

9. A community support system should be established to assist rapid integration of newcomers into the community and revitalize interest by long-time residents in community affairs. A survey, similar to The Survey, administered in fall of 1978, should indicate: 1) a higher percentage of long-time residents and Rock Springs and Green River residents perceive that the quality of life in the community is improving; 2) 25-30 percent of respondents should regard "neighborhood" or "community" as one of the most rewarding aspects of life in Sweetwater County; 3) on a comparison of services (such as that listed in Table B-XII, Appendix B), recreation facilities, friendliness of and acceptance by the community, a place to raise children, community planning, parks, responsiveness of local government, and outdoor recreation should all be ranked "better" by a majority of respondents; and 4) the county average score on Harris' Alienation Scale would be 2.2, with minimal variance between newcomers and long-time residents.

10. There should be general agreement between local government and industry on common (or compatible) legislative lobbying programs on matters of local concern

51

(e.g., the package of bills proposed by the Ostlund Committee, a decision on whether to establish a medical school in Wyoming, passage of the proposed Uniform Intoxication and Treatment Act).

This is not a complete list of objectives—that is the responsibility of local officials and interested citizens. The crucial factor is to make them detailed and specific enough to plan for, to budget for, and to achieve. Since the most important objectives may be the most difficult to express *and* to accomplish, it is important to give serious attention to all of those chosen.

PROGRAM PACKAGE

Program packages to achieve each objective should be prepared, and should be reviewed yearly. Part of the review process is for revision, to deal with what's new. Part is for evaluation, to see how the program is going and what else must be done.

Two examples of program packages are described below.

HOUSING PROGRAM PACKAGE IN RESPONSE TO DETAILED OPERATIONAL OBJECTIVE NO. 2

New legislation required to achieve this objective includes:

1. The Wyoming Community Development Authority bill (Senate File No. 12, 1975), which should be passed with its "loans to lenders" provision.

2. The Bureau of Land Management (BLM) Organic Act, now pending before Congress, should be enacted in a form reinstating the 1964 Act authorizing sale of government lands to municipalities (and/or local housing authorities) for resale for housing development in certain areas.*

---

*Such legislation would permit municipalities to add to the *supply* of land for housing and also to limit its *price*. During the Ft. McMurray, Alberta, boom, the provincial government has released predeveloped land as demand forces prices up beyond the reach of local home buyers. The released land in each case is located adjacent to developed land, facilitating orderly development. Municipal purchase (and predevelopment) of raw land from private sources could have the same effect.

52

3. Wyoming should adopt legislation setting up a county-
    wide regulatory group controlling annexations and the
    formation of cities and new special districts. It
    would be similar to California's Local Agency Forma-
    tion Commission (LAFCO) for ". . . discouragement of
    urban sprawl and the encouragement of the orderly
    formation of local government agencies based upon lo-
    cal conditions and circumstances."*

Assuming that these are enacted, with strong lobbying support from the Sweetwater County community, there are several phases in the process of reaching the objective.

Planning, land acquisition, predevelopment, and early
financing. An early choice must be between annexable
scattered developments, a single annexable development, or
a socially and economically cohesive new community. Any
of these can theoretically offer the tangible and intangible amenities necessary for satisfactory quality of life
during a period of growth and in-migration. A satellite,
or housing-only suburb, lacking public and commercial facilities, is unlikely to offer this basis for community
integration. The wholly new community may have similar
problems unless it is complete. Access to employment and
service centers and to existing utilities will affect both
public and private costs.

The town of Green River may already have available the
land needed for the first year's increment of houses from
its early BLM purchase. Other sources include Upland Industries, the Westerly development, other private land-
owners, and BLM land if it is again made available through
the revised Organic Act.

Land acquisition or assembly may be financed by a developer, by a consortium of lenders, or with the participation of local industrial firms (which may or may not be
interested in subsidizing the acquisition or controlling
the cost of the land).

Predevelopment may be partially financed by the proposed
Wyoming Community Development Authority if land is annexed
and the utilities and streets are built as public facilities. Wyoming Farm Loan Board funds can be used for water,
sewage, and solid waste facilities via the Joint Powers
Act. More conventionally, predevelopment may be financed
by the developer.

Front end financing for construction may be obtained from
private lenders, or from industrial firms concerned with
the quality of life in Sweetwater County.

---

*California Government Code Section 46774, 1963.

Purchase financing. If 7½ percent purchase financing is available from the Wyoming Community Development Authority (or some other source), a $35,000 house* (stick-built or manufactured) can be bought with a $3,000 down payment and $225 monthly payments--this may or may not meet the price limitation in the detailed operational objective for housing. An alternative is direct subsidy of housing construction, purchase, or rental by industry or government (a Sweetwater County Housing Authority may be helpful). The problem of financing the equally vital housing for local service employees with lower income, who cannot afford the down payment or the monthly payments, will remain. Other alternatives for lowering the purchase price include incomplete interior finishing and little or no landscaping (although the latter is considered highly important, according to The Survey, Appendix B).

Employers may finance second mortgages to assist their employees with down payments. They could also sell housing to their employees on a purchase contract, with employer buyback of the employee's equity, adjusted for inflation, if the employee leaves the employer.† Both are alternatives that allow employees of large firms to buy housing.

The remaining 20 percent of the housing units to meet the quota will presumably be higher priced housing, conventionally financed. Mobile home spaces will probably be adequately available as construction employment drops off. The poorer mobile home parks will then suffer competition from better facilities, and all are likely to be upgraded by stronger local enforcement of zoning, health, and building standards.

HOUSING PROGRAM PACKAGE FINANCIAL NOTES

The order of magnitude of financial requirements for 1975 for this undertaking, based on both the 1978 high population estimates and the 1978 conservative estimates (Table I), are as follows.

---

*Building costs are estimated to be in the $23-28 per square foot range, based on 1974 experience of one builder in the Rocky Mountain Region.

†A similar plan is in effect in Ft. McMurray, Alberta.

54

	High Estimate	Conservative Estimate
Permanent housing units needed in 1975, to meet the 1978 requirement	1,000	500
Units requiring financial assistance	800	400
Cost of developed land (raw land at $1,500-3,000/ acre and utilities, including treatment plants plus collection and distribution	$10-15 million	$5-7.5 million
Other public facilities and buildings (including schools)	$2-8 million (these costs depend on access to existing facilities with spare capacity)	$1-4 million
Construction financing (private)	$2-5 million	$2-4 million
Purchase financing (WCDA loans to lenders for 7½ percent mortgages)	$26 million*	$13 million

---

*The funds needed from the proposed Wyoming Community Development Authority for just the first year of a three-year program for Sweetwater County make up a substantial part of its proposed $100 million bonding capacity. It is possible that the 20 percent local service housing described in the Housing Program Package might qualify for assistance under Section 8 of the Housing and Community Development Act of 1974 for annual contributions for moderate income families to *rent* housing if the Department of Housing and Urban Development clarifies its regulations, and if funds are available to Wyoming or from the Secretary's discretionary funds. Additionally, the Farmers Home Administration is a source of both home ownership and public facilities loans and its authorizations were extended by the Community Development Act of 1974.

1. Countywide outreach campaign

2. Countywide recreation program

3. Expanded communication role for electronic media

4. Western Wyoming College expansion of adult education
   and career development opportunities

   Background. The growth management model described in
Chapter 2 defined quality of life in terms of tangible el-
ements (adequacy of goods and services available and affordable in the local services sector) and intangible ele-
ments (supportive spirit of the community, responsive government, and adequate leisure time activities). While
detailed operational objectives one through seven deal
primarily with the tangible aspects of quality of life,
eight and nine attempt to achieve and measure improvement
in the intangible aspects of quality of life.

Alienation (as determined by The Survey) is the feeling of
powerlessness to change one's environment. It was consistently related to individual mobility, and was minimal
in people with high involvement in community activities.
For example, individuals who expected to remain in the
area for only a short time had higher than average scores.
Highly mobile individuals (i.e., those who have moved a
number of times in the last few years) had the highest
alienation scores of any subgroup analyzed, while individuals who have never moved had very low alienation scores.
This merely emphasizes the fact that many people who move
often never "put down roots" which allow them to become
established in a community and have a voice in its direction.

Personal satisfaction with life is directly related to
alienation. Survey respondents with low alienation scores
exhibited the highest level of satisfaction of any subgroup analyzed. High levels of personal contentment were
also found among individuals who expect to remain in the
area for the rest of their lives, long-time residents, and
people who consider themselves to be highly involved in
community affairs.

These results indicate that a program package designed to
achieve detailed operational objectives eight and nine
should emphasize expanding opportunities for attaining a
high degree of personal satisfaction among Sweetwater
County residents. The feeling of permanence--of having
"put down roots" in the community--appears to be crucial
to this. Availability of permanent housing increases the
perception of permanence among individuals. Involvement
in community affairs not only helps to keep an individual

and family in the community, but also increases the sense of personal worth and satisfaction.

Involvement and integration in the community may be expressed in various ways, from friendly "across the back fence" visits with neighbors to campaigning for elected office. An initial program package designed to keep people in the community active and satisfied might contain the following components: a countywide outreach campaign, a countywide recreation program, an expanded communications role for electronic media, and an expansion of the adult education and career development opportunities at Western Wyoming College. These components are designed to augment one another; for each to be most successful they must all be implemented together.

1. *A countywide outreach program* would serve several purposes: it would inform residents of services and activities available in the community, attract new members to volunteer organizations, and encourage formation of new friendships.

A telephone referral service providing information on social services available in the community (health care, babysitting, family counseling, suicide prevention, etc.), and also on which government agency to contact for specific problems (trash collection, employment, welfare) should be established and publicized widely and regularly. A complete listing of leisure time activities—recreation programs and facilities, volunteer civic associations, cultural, religious, and educational groups—should also be available.

Often a community center, or the need for one, acts as a stimulus to formation of neighborhood organizations. Government planning efforts to identify neighborhoods and work with people in each area often give rise to neighborhood associations. These associations are effective catalysts for citizen involvement and feelings of community identification.

Major employers in the area can facilitate the integration of newcomers with orientation sessions that bring together old and new employees and their families. Picnics, interindustry team sports, bridge clubs, and "partners" approach to orienting new employees (including wives' partnerships) all assist integration efforts. Employers might also recognize community involvement on the part of employees by giving awards for special efforts such as coaching a little league team, leading a youth group, serving on the cancer drive committee, or volunteer tutoring.

The outreach program might also feature a coordinated membership drive of all volunteer organizations in the county, including civic organizations (Women's Club, League of Women Voters, Junior Chamber of Commerce), cultural, recreational, and hobby clubs (theater groups, museum memberships, garden club, gun club, snowmobilers), and service organizations (Parent-Teacher Association, Kiwanis, church groups, Girl or Boy Scouts, Red Cross). Every group should join together in a month-long, well-publicized campaign to generate interest and new members. Such a drive might even prompt people to organize a new club or group, such as a volunteer probation officer program or perhaps a Gray Panthers group.

Volunteerism offers a unique opportunity for personal satisfaction, and simultaneously meets otherwise unattended community needs. Federal funding is available through ACTION to encourage and coordinate volunteer activities in a community. One program of particular interest to Sweetwater County is ACTION Technical Assistance, through which federal funds are available for matching volunteers who have special technical expertise with small business or not-for-profit organizational needs.

The county might also consider funding establisment of a Commission on Community Relations. Citizen advisory committees to such a commission would examine new approaches to creating a personally satisfying quality of life for Sweetwater residents. To examine alternatives and report their findings, the CAC might use the porta-pak community television approach described in component 3.

2. *A countywide recreation program* should be established. The Priorities Board Citizens Advisory Committee should establish a volunteer task force to prepare a program package for attaining detailed operational objective eight.* This objective is a long-range goal. It will require both public and private investment, and might take a variety of forms.† The program package therefore will require consideration of incentives to private entrepreneurs, use of industrial development bonds, and so on.

---

*Again, a well-advertised request for volunteers would give otherwise uninvolved residents an opportunity to participate in a personally relevant project.

†If, for instance, private entrepreneurs opened a restaurant/lounge in Green River or a large recreational complex, it would help to achieve DOO 8, but would not reduce the need for continued public planning toward parks, community centers, tennis courts, etc.

The task force might also prepare an interim plan for recreation and leisure time activities to be completed by May
1975 for presentation at the county budget hearings. If
the county would take the initiative to form a countywide
recreation district, employing staff to organize and direct recreational programs for the entire population, an
effective program could be in operation by fall of 1975.
The Wyoming Recreation Commission might fund part of this.
With full-time staff available to assure maintenance and
protection of facilities, more extensive public use of existing facilities would be possible. For example, school
gymnasiums could be opened for adult sports, and/or church
basements might substitute as youth centers.

A recreation director would initiate activities such as
little league or teen clubs and also assume responsibility
for coordination of youth oriented activities with those
for adults (such as bridge tournaments).* Close cooperation with Western Wyoming College in planning activities
such as yoga classes, volleyball tournaments, sewing clubs,
and so on would be mutually beneficial.

A countywide program would also allow the staff to build a
constituency. As people became more involved and new activities were begun, they might be motivated to seek private support for building new facilities to help achieve
detailed operational objective eight.

   3. *The various electronic media (video and audio)
should have a role in fostering community commitment.* A
number of communities throughout the United States and
Canada are experimenting with innovative uses of the electronic media to foster such interest and involvement. The
key to these activities is feedback--reaction, comment,
criticism, and participation. Feedback mechanisms allow
local residents to react to the material that is presented.
This feedback influences future programming and assures
relevance to the local population.

Broader application of existing local cable systems and
radio stations as a community resource might include locally originated programming from Western Wyoming College,
such as seminars with guest speakers, classes such as

---

*In group interviews with women, complaints surfaced
regarding the difficulty of successfully organizing youth
activities such as little league. However, it was pointed
out that usually these efforts concentrated on children
but did nothing to bring the parents into community life.
A program director would be concerned with the participation of all family members in a wide variety of activities.

handicrafts or mechanics, and student theater productions. Social service agencies (public and private) might produce informational programs describing their activities. City council and county commission meetings might be broadcast. The Sweetwater County Historical Society could offer programs on past history of the county. These programs should be carried on the cable systems and, wherever appropriate, telephone feedback should be included.

A community videotaping project could be undertaken as an extension of these other activities. Such a project could be done using the portable video-tape camera (porta-pak) which permits easy production of television-type pictures. The porta-pak is easy to operate, relatively inexpensive equipment which allows the amateur to visit the "nooks and crannies" of the community, interview individuals or groups, and produce tapes (the contents of which may vary from the secret of Chinese cooking to survival in the desert). The tapes are then reproduced on local television stations, cable systems, or individual home sets.*

As an initial project, a community videotaping effort might develop a Sweetwater County community profile designed to: introduce newcomers and old-timers to each other; share different perspectives on the community and its needs; get reaction to these perspectives; put perspectives and reactions together in visual documents; inform and entertain both the participants and the audience attracted by the localized video material; and begin the community objective-setting-by-consensus process. The project would have local citizens pooling their talents and interests to picture their views of Sweetwater County and their concerns.

The creation of these visual documents and the reactions to them in public meetings or in telephone conversations between viewers, producers, and commentators is a new experience in assembling diverse ideas from various people. Both the creation of a video community profile (or a document on a single issue) and the subsequent discussion generate intense interest. Experience elsewhere in the U.S. and Canada indicates that response and participation grow, including many who previously took no part in local activities. There are two prerequisites for such a program: equipment and training, supportable by a grant from industry or the Wyoming Council for the Humanities, probably to Western Wyoming College; and an operating base and sponsorship, such as Western Wyoming College. Sponsorship might be shared with a volunteer association in the county.

_____

*A schoolroom, library, neighborhood bar, or an individual's home may become a community viewing center when the porta-pak video tape is shown to groups via a home television set.

60

4. *Adult education and career development opportunities at Western Wyoming College should be expanded.* The College provides unique opportunities as a center for increasing personal satisfaction. Survey results indicated that 35 percent of respondents were "extremely interested" or "quite interested" in attending classes there. Newcomers and respondents who expected to remain in the area one to five years showed the greatest interest.

A countywide bus system should be in operation soon, and the planned day-care center (also offering services in the evenings) should be constructed and available as soon as possible. The county might consider leasing three or four minibuses to service Green River, Superior, Reliance, and outlying areas with schedules coinciding with heavy demand for classes. A cooperative babysitting pool of students--coordinated through the College--might also encourage attendance for women.*

A further role for the College is suggested by the lag in buildup of private local services, and women's dissatisfaction with career opportunities in the county.† If the College were to undertake an active business management program and recruit women for it, some of these women might go on to open small business operations in the county. Front end money might be provided by a Sweetwater County equity fund, and other capital from the sale of Wyoming Industrial Development Bonds.

The long term goal of this program package is an enriched quality of life for Sweetwater residents. Measuring success will often be difficult, even with surveys, since the objective cannot be quantified. Also, much of its success depends on individual enthusiasm and participation--and this cannot be legislated.

It is thought, however, that simultaneous initiation of 1) the process of developing and discussing a Sweetwater

---

*According to The Survey, aside from lack of free time, the major inhibitors to attendance were poor driving conditions, inadequate transportation, and lack of babysitting facilities. These difficulties reinforce the idea of using the College as a center for the community video concept to reduce the need for transportation services. In a "Know Your Neighbor Program" residents of the outlying areas could produce their own tapes for distribution and discussion in Rock Springs and Green River, and vice versa.

†The Survey indicated that women in the rural areas ranked second in high alienation scores.

County community profile, 2) a membership drive to recruit new members to volunteer associations, 3) greater access to College services, and 4) a countywide recreation program, will create a snowballing effect of community involvement leading to increased personal satisfaction.

The complexity of the objective and the variety of programs suggest that the Priorities Board should consider hiring a Director of Community Development as the first step in achieving an enriched quality of life. This person would coordinate and monitor the quality of life programs, and would deal with the program leadership, the Priorities Board, and others financing the program.

ENHANCING THE INTANGIBLE ASPECTS OF THE QUALITY OF LIFE—FINANCIAL NOTES

The order of magnitude of financial requirements for this undertaking for a single year follows. These are annual operating costs, with no capital investment immediately required (except as noted).

Telephone referral service	$ 55,000
Neighborhood planning personnel in existing planning offices	35,000
Selective grants to organizations for membership drives	10,000
Commission on community relations	35,000
Recreation program for utilizing existing facilities	115,000
Electronic media program (includes one-time cost of $25,000 for equipment)	65,000
Western Wyoming College programs	200,000
Equity funding for small businesses (repayable grants)	50,000
Director of Community Development	45,000
	$610,000

An agenda for decision-making indicates the order in which decisions should be made. The forecasts of employment* and population in Chapter 1 specify assumptions about the future. The hierarchy of objectives states what *is* desired. The program packages describe the *specific means* of reaching the objectives. The agenda is a reminder that decisions will be taking place over *time*, with different accomplishments requiring differing amounts of lead time.

Some of the data, circumstances, and decisions which would need to be considered if the objectives described earlier were actually chosen by local consensus, are listed below.

Agenda for Decision Making

Year: 1976

1. Review the functioning and the organizational structure of the Sweetwater County Priorities Board. Is it more than just a conduit for information and grant requests? Is it operating to coordinate efforts to solve countywide problems? Is it assisting in generating and maintaining consensus?

2. Subject to the approval of the Local Agency Formation Commission, site selection and required zoning changes for 2,500 units of permanent housing should be completed. Site selection and zoning changes required for an additional 1,500 units (required by 1978) will have begun.

3. The county land use plan to be submitted to Wyoming Land Use Commission should be near completion. Given extensive population spill-over into adjoining counties (both in permanent residents and use of recreational resources) a regional planning group should have been established to develop the plan. On a continuing basis this group (intercounty planning council) might develop a comprehensive growth management plan for projected population increases. The Office of Management and Budget Circular A-95 review process, requiring intergovernmental review of grant applications, and the Joint Powers Act, will both encourage sharing of resources. The growth management plan would be a regional plan which includes land use, transportation, environmental quality, recreation use, and projected revenues.

4. Update the five year budget plan submitted to Priorities Board in 1975.

    *The forecast and the alternative sets of assumptions affecting future employment should be critically reviewed and revised every other year.

63

5. The community will find it necessary to decide if it wants an air quality maintenance region designation which will encourage or discourage further industrial development (assuming that the November 1974 regulations of the Environmental Protection Agency are maintained).

6. It may be desirable to request a project of the University of Wyoming which will identify or develop strains of grass and plants suitable for landscaping and green space in the Sweetwater County environment. Token funding by the community may be needed.

7. The Priorities Board should monitor community development efforts in the Powder River Basin, in southeast Montana, in the Colorado-Utah oil shale and coal developments, in the North Dakota lignite fields, and in the Four Corners coal development, as these areas compete with Sweetwater County for mining and construction labor.

8. Land acquisition programs for recreational needs after further growth should be underway.

9. Forecasts for growth in economic activity and population should be reviewed.

10. If imbalance between school districts in assessed valuation continues, planning for consolidation should be undertaken.

11. With higher bonding capacities available (and being used), review of debt structure and costs should be maintained. Operating budgets should be studied. A tax structure covering the costs of growth and equitably distributing the costs may be the subject of a new operating objective.

12. If growth forecasts are still comparable to those of 1974, a comprehensive transportation study should be undertaken to provide for the early 1980s population. It should include recommendations for revenues and implementation.

13. A decision on issuing permits for a fifth trona plant to begin construction will be necessary. It should be based on the local community's ability to accommodate new employees.

14. Expansion of the Sweetwater Counseling Services program "Counseling to Aid Women in Distress" may require additional funding.

15. Lobbying at the state level has succeeded in establishment of mobile home standards and an increase in assessment of mobile homes.

Growth Management Agenda for Decision Making

Year: 1978	Conservative Estimate	High Estimate
Plants: under construction:	one new trona	same, plus fifth unit of Jim Bridger
operating:	four trona one coal	one additional coal mine
Employment: construction:	1,600	3,600
(Total) plant:	4,450	4,575
local service:	8,940	10,600
Population: Total:	39,943	48,873
school children:	11,305	13,741
Total school rooms required:	452	550
Incremental school rooms required:	37	98
Total permanent housing units required:	6,146	6,878
Incremental permanent housing units required:	2,697	3,429
Incremental mobile home pads required:	212	337
Estimated revenues to county from *ad valorem* tax on trona, coal production	?	?
Estimated revenues from property tax (residential, commercial, industrial)	?	?
Estimated bonding capacity for* Rock Springs	?	?
Green River	?	?
School districts one and two	?	?
County	?	?

*Assumes state has increased bonding limit by 1975 legislative recommendations, i.e., passage of a constitutional amendment doubling the debt limit of cities, counties, and school districts.

Agenda for Decision Making

Year: 1979

1. Review the functioning of the Sweetwater County Priorities Board (as in 1976).

2. Green River and Rock Springs city governments should be self-sufficient in planning and administrative staff.

3. The development of the recreation complexes should be reviewed. If they are not meeting community objectives, public facilities and programs should be expanded.

4. Basic to local service employment multipliers should be reviewed to see if they have met the 1975 detailed operational objective (a return approximately to 1971 levels).

5. The transportation plan authorized in 1976 should be in the early stages of implementation.

6. As coal and trona mining and processing grow to further dominate the Sweetwater County economy, active efforts to diversify the economy should be considered. These would probably involve trade-off decisions between seeking diversification and thus generating more growth or maintaining a specialized mining economy dependent on changes in technology or markets. A successful diversification program would probably require six to ten years, so advance planning is necessary.

7. The Priorities Board (in conjunction with the inter-county planning council) has established guidelines for industrial entry or expansion in the area, including provision of housing for some proportion of new employees brought to the area.

8. Survey (completed in 1978) results indicating achievement of detailed operational objective #9 should guide further efforts to enrich the quality of life.

9. The hierarchy of goals and objectives should be examined and, if necessary, revised and reordered.

Growth Management Agenda for Decision Making

Year: 1983		Conservative Estimate	Moderate Estimate	High Estimate
Plants:	under construction:	one new trona	Same as conservative plus 1 coal gasification or liquefaction	Same as moderate plus intensive coal development and oil shale
	operating:	five trona two coal		
Employment: (Total)	construction:	1,000	4,000	5,000
	plant:	7,300	8,900	10,700
	local service:	11,760	16,450	18,000
Population:	Total:	53,395	76,870	88,875
	school children:	15,281	21,826	25,380
Total school rooms required:		611	873	1,015
Incremental school rooms required:		61	262	142
Total permanent housing units required:		9,935		15,876
Incremental permanent housing units required:		3,789	8,566	8,998
Incremental mobile home pads required:		323	1,316	1,124
Estimated revenues to county from *ad valorem* tax on trona, coal, power production		?	?	?
Estimated revenues from property tax (residential, commercial, industrial)		?	?	?
Estimated bonding capacity for*				
Rock Springs		?	?	?
Green River		?	?	?
School districts one and two		?	?	?
County		?	?	?

---

*Assumes state has increased bonding limit by 1975 legislative recommendations, i.e., passage of a constitutional amendment doubling debt limit of cities, counties, and school districts.

APPENDIXES

Several new problem solving arrangements, organizations, or processes are needed to handle the boom in Sweetwater County (or to handle similar situations elsewhere).

Local government and industry need to work together to deal with problems resulting from industrial growth and which interfere with industrial profitability.

A Wyoming Development Corporation should be established to help provided needed housing and public facilities, along with other governmental tools.

Both the State of Wyoming and local governments need a greater growth management capability.

The remainder of this section will describe concepts for each of these new institutions, and will also suggest specific remedies for some of the problems described in the section What Are the Boom Problems?

THE PRIORITIES BOARD (THE FERRERO PLAN)

One of the most urgent needs is a mechanism for Sweetwater County local government and industry to get together for problem solving.† County Commissioner Dominick Ferrero has suggested the following plan.

---

*From working paper, August 1974.

†Neighboring counties, facing similar growth problems, may also wish to establish priorities boards. As they do, joint meetings or meetings of representatives from each board would appear to be desirable to better deal with shared problems.

A Sweetwater County Priorities Board would be authorized
and established by the county commissioners and the city
governments of Rock Springs and Green River. The board
would consist of:

1. The chairman and one other county commissioner.

2. The mayor and one other official from each town (Rock
    Springs and Green River).

3. Two representatives of industry.*

4. Two representatives selected at large (chosen by the
    elected officials).

The purpose of the board would be fourfold:

1. To provide regular communication between local gov-
    ernment and industry on information and plans of mu-
    tual interest.

2. To analyze current and future local problems and rec-
    ommend priorities for their solution.

3. Short-range--to work out coordinated proposals for
    industry help in solving boom problems, the help to
    be furnished in lobbying support, manpower, or money,
    as appropriate; and to coordinate approaches to Wyo-
    ming state government for related assistance.

4. Long-range--to move toward economic self-sufficiency
    for local government and an adequate capability for
    managing the growth of Sweetwater County.

The board would meet at least bi-monthly. Wyoming state
government observers would be invited from such agencies
as the Department of Economic Planning and Development,
the Highway Department, and others. Representatives from
the Federal Regional Council in Denver might also be invited.

The board would be advised by a citizens' advisory committee and a technical committee. The citizens' committee
would include representatives from chambers of commerce,
League of Women Voters, and other interest groups. The
technical committee would include planners, engineers,
health administrators, educators, and other specialists
from the community.†

---

*These might be recommended by an industry associa-
tion to represent the mining and energy companies, the
railroad, and (probably) Upland Industries.

†School district representation may be required on
the board, rather than in an advisory role.

Probably no formal relationship with the Sweetwater County
legislative delegation is necessary, but it would be desirable to keep them fully acquainted with the board's activities.

HOUSING AND PUBLIC FACILITIES: A WYOMING DEVELOPMENT CORPORATION

There are several ways to attack the housing and public
facilities problem. Any combination of the alternatives
listed below would help Sweetwater County "catch up" to
demand and meet future demand in a more timely and planned
fashion.

The development corporation. The idea of a housing
development corporation has been suggested in several different variations, ranging from a county housing authority
to a state community development corporation similar to
New York State's Urban Development Corporation. However,
an authority dealing only with housing is not sufficient;
we would recommend a community development corporation.

A community development corporation would be responsible
for planning and financing housing as well as other public
facilities and services such as water, sanitation, school
buildings, and possibly recreation. It should be a free
wheeling enterprise with authority to furnish capital and
entrepreneurial help to local governments. It should be
able to issue revenue bonds, match grants from federal
government, attract private investment from corporations,
guarantee loans and subsidize interest, and purchase residential mortgages.* It might consider developing its own

---

*The best known such agency is the New York Urban De-
velopment Corporation:

    The New York State Urban Development Corporation has
    far broader powers concerning land acquisition and
    development than have been granted by any other state.
    It has the power to acquire real property by purchase,
    lease, or condemnation, and to develop projects with-
    out conforming to local zoning ordinances, local
    zoning codes, or local laws or regulations when com-
    pliance is not feasible or practical. UDC may exer-
    cise this power directly or through subsidiary corp-
    orations to which it can make loans. In addition, the
    enabling law grants UDC projects full or partial ex-
    emption from local real property taxes, except for
    assessments for local improvements.
        Thus, the UDC has the full range of development
    powers, and can do everything a state housing finance
    agency can do (except for mortgage insurance and sec-
    ondary mortgage activities). The UDC can acquire

73

construction work force to go into an area, set up mobile home units until the first homes are built, and continue living there as construction proceeds. This would assure consistency in standards of quality, and solve some labor market and cost problems. The corporation could become self-supporting after an initial (probably five years) period of operation subsidized by the state or by industry.

Financing. The establishment of a development gains tax (tax on the *net* capital gain from sale of real estate) could at once reduce land price speculation and be a new source of funding for the development corporation. Minerals severance taxes, revenue sharing, and other state sources could also be used.

The trona companies have demonstrated a concern and willingness to help in providing housing to date. They might consider providing seed money to a development corporation which might become self-sustaining. The corporation might also be an appropriate vehicle through which companies might channel subsidies for housing and facilities.

---

land, hire architects and engineers, choose builders and developers, arrange subsidies, issue building permits, make mortgage loans, conduct closings, and perform other related services.

Whereas most HFA development activities are limited to residential projects, the UDC is not. It can also develop land for commercial and industrial purposes, as well as for public facilities. The corporation has constructed a municipal parking garage, a convention center, an office building, and an industrial park. It has begun to become involved in large-scale development projects and is developing three new communities around the State, including one on Welfare Island in New York City.

The UDC, founded in 1968, has constructed over 30,000 units of housing costing an estimated $1.2 billion; its bonding capacity is $1.5 billion. (Stevens, *Wyoming Housing Alternatives*, Vol. II, Cheyenne: DEPAD, 1974.)

The Illinois Housing Development Authority recently established a pilot program in which it may sell tax exempt securities and lend the proceeds to savings and loan associations and banks that agree to match the funds with an equal amount of loans in their primary service area (area in which 60 percent of the institution's savings and time deposits are located). Institutions may borrow up to the amount of conventional mortgage loans made in their area the preceding year. With the matching funds, loans can be made to finance single family homes of up to $35,000 or apartments of up to $70,000.

74

Zoning and building permits. Zoning ordinances can
also be useful. In Boulder, Colorado, and in some cities
of California, municipalities have legislated a 10-20 percent requirement for low and moderate income housing in
any new subdivision. In Lakewood and Aurora, Colorado,
the number of new units of low and moderate income housing
that a developer must provide is negotiated at the time a
building permit is issued. Some cities experiencing boom
growth have required developers to provide not only the
land for schools, but also the building--which is then
dedicated to the school district.

Building permit fees also give the county or city an opportunity to recover some of the cost of development. If
the fee is based on the present value of the stream of
future costs of support services, the necessity for tax
increases is reduced.

> Using again the example of 7,000 people being added
> to the population with $40,000,000 of additional
> assessed valuation, this would add 275 school child-
> ren and $5.7 million in valuation per 1,000 new in-
> habitants. The *average* cost of education per child
> in the Rock Springs District 1 in 1973-74 was $1,199.
> Of this, $1,018 was locally raised revenue--the rest
> was from the state. However, a 42 mill combined
> district and county school levy would only raise $870
> per student, an annual deficit of $148, or $1,480
> over ten years. The present value of that $1,480
> ten-year deficit is $570, discounting at ten percent.
> Discounting at six percent (the district's cost of
> capital), the present value is $826.

Some such per student deficit present value charge, covering the prospective operating deficit of the school, might
be legislatively incorporated into the building permit
structure, with the proceeds to be turned over to the
school district.

Employer assurance of housing. Another possibility
is that new employers in the area be required to provide
housing and a portion of public facilities construction
costs for their employees *before* coming into the area.
This might include a phasing of mobile homes for construction workers to permanent housing for permanent employees.
Any new housing built by a company for its employees might
be rented and possibly subsidized until that employee can
afford to purchase it (if he so desires). Thus, an option
to buy is an incentive to the employee to remain with his
current employer; and a homeowning employee may be less
apt to move from the local labor market.

BLM land. Under the 1964 Land Sales Act, the Bureau
of Land Management was permitted to sell land to municipalities at noncompetitive prices for housing development.
This legislation expired in 1970 but needs to be rein-
stated.

Presently, under the BLM Recreation and Public Purposes
Act, any non-profit group may purchase land for $2.50 per
acre as long as its use is kept in public ownership. The
establishment of a county housing authority would allow
such purchases. Under the Section 23 Lease Program
(which is presently the only source of federal support for
low and moderate income housing), a housing authority is a
prerequisite to funding.

Mobile homes. Mobile homes are an alternative; however, if mobile homes are to be utilized, they should meet
the same quality standards as site homes. Strict subdivision regulations, including water and sanitation standards,
trash collection, roads and space separations, are essential. Staffing of the county planning office to enforce
standards is also essential. A particular need in Wyoming
is higher specifications for mobile home construction to
reduce fire hazard.

A GREATER CAPABILITY FOR GROWTH MANAGEMENT

The previous section on Housing and Public Facilities
listed a number of means for handling one aspect of growth
management, the provision of housing and public facilities.
Similarly, several tools (including those just described)
are needed for management of growth itself.

The variables of growth. Four crucial variables must
be addressed to manage economic growth if the problems described earlier are to be solved or avoided:

1. Where should the growth be located?

2. What should the rate of growth be?

3. How should the benefits of growth be shared?

4. How should the costs of growth be paid for, and who
    should pay them?

Objectives for growth management. Generalized goals
for growth management are easily identified; for instance,
most public policy and legislation is justified as being
necessary for the public health, safety, and welfare.
Only slightly more specific are good intentions like
maintaining the quality of life, supporting industrial
productivity, or preserving choice of life style.

For growth management purposes, specific objectives must
be set. They must be specific enough to tell if they have
been achieved (or are being achieved). "Adequate housing"
is not specific; "construction and availability of 2,400
units of housing by 1977, at least one third of them rent-
als at a rental cost of not over 20 percent of the average
trona miner's monthly earnings" is more specific.

Objective setting, with objectives stated in specific, operational form, is the first requisite for managing growth.
Only after that can policy be determined, priorities set,
new tools developed, and programs designed and budgeted.
The objectives have to come first.

Tools for growth management. A few are already
available, like county and city planning and zoning,
building permits, and some subdivision authority. Some
environmental protection authority is now available.
These are police power tools.

They should be supplemented by more extensive subdivision,
annexation, and new town controls, by legislation requiring all development to conform to a local comprehensive plan (which specifies maximum growth rates). With
these, more cohesive and contiguous residential development could be achieved, instead of the recent leapfrogging,
scattered developments. Plant site control legislation
should be enacted requiring advance notice of construction
of industrial operations employing a minimum number of employees, e.g., 150, plus the filing of a community development impact statement and conformity to the comprehensive plan.

Growth management cannot be done only by the police power.
The forces of the market also should be directed to this
end. Where the market is not working, as with housing, it
should be stimulated. Public or semi-public investment,
by a development corporation or by a local government en-
tity (such as Green River's obtaining of BLM land for
housing) should be fostered.

Where an attractive market situation (e.g., soda ash, coal,
land speculation) exists, the public and social costs of
sudden growth to meet that market should be internalized
into those market transactions. This may require constant
reevaluation of state tax policy toward boom growth industries; it may require more taxing (and assessment) flexibility for local government, including authorization of a
local income tax.

In either case, the goal should be to make local government economically self-sufficient, independent of special
grants from industry, and able to service the growth that
meets growth management objectives.

Phasing into growth management. Once the problems are identified (or forecast), objective-setting can start. The Priorities Board proposed earlier may have a most important role in this. Then a ten-year, year-by-year agenda of problems and needed decisions (including identification of needed legislation) should be prepared and revised annually.

SPECIFIC REMEDIES

The three concepts just described address most of the issues identified earlier, as shown in Table A-I. In addition, some remedies are suggested here for specific boom problems described earlier.

TABLE A-I

Concepts vs. Issues

Issue	I Priorities Board	II Wyoming Development Corporation	III Growth Management Capability
Housing and public facilities	X	XX	X
Fringe settlements	X	X	XX
Labor market			X
Spouse problems	X		
Government structures	XX	X	XX
Land oligopoly	X	XX	X
Urban problems	X	X	XX
Industry-government cooperation	XX	X	
Specialized economy	X	X	X
Growth rates	X		XX

  X Covers issue to some extent.
XX Addresses issue directly.

Health services. A new institution for furnishing comprehensive health care, a health maintenance organization (HMO), is starting to enroll members. Sweetwater Health Services, Inc., the HMO, is set up by local physicians, with federal assistance, to offer prepaid health care. It emphasizes preventive medicine and does not require hospitalization before it pays for physicians' services. It has already proven useful in bringing needed health service personnel to Sweetwater County and in organizing local health resources to meet health care crises. It offers the hope of making the best use of health resources in years to come.

Major employers should endorse the HMO and offer it as an alternative form of health insurance as soon as possible. They also should examine its opportunities to expand or speed up its development and consider making grants to enlarge its programs.

Recreation. If and as bond issues for recreation facilities are offered, they merit broad support. In the meantime, consideration should be given to a countywide recreation program which would employ recreation specialists and the necessary administrative, maintenance, and custodial personnel to permit using and maintaining school recreational facilities for year-around public use.

Corporate and county support of this program would help in its adoption and continuation and could reduce the need for either public or private investment in recreation facilities. Corporate support of an expanded Western Wyoming College adult education and cultural activities program could serve the same purposes.

Educational facilities. This problem has already been discussed at length. Another approach to avoiding the Wyoming constitutional limit on school bonding involves legislative action to raise the schools' property tax mill levy limits so they could lease school buildings. The buildings could be financed and built by a state-authorized development corporation (using tax exempt bonds), or by locally operating industrial corporations, using their own funds, or by a nonprofit corporation set up by the industrial corporations.

Problems of women. The Sweetwater County job market is dominated by men's jobs. Because of this and many of the quality of life problems already enumerated, many of the wives of employed men lead unusually frustrating existences.

The first remedy is solution of the quality of life problems already enumerated. Wives are affected by all of them. Beyond that, two remedies are needed: 1) the newcomer wife should be actively welcomed to the community, and 2) the resident wife should be given a greater variety of ways to spend her time.

For the first, an outreach program to contact families moving into town should be funded by industry (not just one company). It should adapt the Welcome Wagon concept of furnishing information on public and private services,

79

schools, churches, shopping, health care, and leisure time activities. It should seek out newly arrived wives and let them feel that someone knows they exist. The service may grow to include a full-time office, and a telephone referral service.

For the resident wife, more industrial jobs will help. So would a source of venture capital for the entrepreneurial woman who wants to open a shop; this would also augment the local service sector of the economy. Education and cultural programs at Western Wyoming College can be expanded and school transportation should be furnished, serving Green River and Point of Rocks. To make these programs usable, child care centers should be established (possibly by the county, possibly by industry) to look after children on either a regular or occasional basis.

Productivity problems. The best solution is that already advanced: to make Sweetwater County a more attractive place to which industrial labor can be attracted and retained. Two additional approaches merit consideration: 1) expand training programs for unskilled people, and 2) with the aid of such programs, tap unused labor pools such as racial minorities living elsewhere or women living in Sweetwater County.

Encouragement of home ownership by local employees may help retention, particularly as job market competition with other Rocky Mountain area minerals employers speeds up.

Viability of local government. A number of areas for industry support of local government are listed in the section of this appendix beginning on page 83. These include issues for legislative lobbying, and specific projects for financial support. One conspicuous need for added local government effort appears to be in the field of planning. Given the nature of the boom problems, annual planning expenditures of $5 to $10 per capita appear appropriate. Additional resources are probably needed for five year budget programming. (The *Rock Springs Community Development Study 1973* is a desirable approach to this.)

It is possible that some planning support could be obtained from the U.S. Economic Development Administration, or directly from the Mountain Plains Federal Regional Council in Denver. Both are supporting planning for a *prospective* boom in Colorado oil shale country; they might do something for an actual boom in Sweetwater County.

Finally, industry also needs to support planning with more information. Strong possibilities of capital investment programs should be discussed with local officials, as well as firm decisions to proceed with new construction. Lead time for public sector decisions is vital.

If the present problems of boom growth are to be solved, growth must be managed. If future growth is to be less disruptive, growth must be managed.

The growth management process starts with defining clear and specific objectives. These must be set by elected officials, with extensive participation by citizens (and interest groups) of the community. The objectives must represent a broad community consensus or it is unlikely that they can ever be achieved. The concept of the Priorities Board may be useful for this.

The next step in the process is implementation. This working paper offers several different concepts and remedies for managing boom growth. Some combination of these, plus others that evolve with study and experience, will help in solving growth problems.

It will require continuing effort by elected officials (and their staffs), private industry, and interested citizens to determine the means for meeting these objectives. It will require even more effort to put objectives and means and interest groups together to manage growth in Sweetwater County.

ASSUMPTIONS ON POPULATION FORECASTS, HOUSING, AND SCHOOLROOM REQUIREMENTS

Table III, page 9, gives the estimated population increases through the early 1980s based on differing employment projections. Total population is derived by estimating family population and adding that to the single population. Family population was calculated by assuming 3.5 people per family unit.

To determine the number of family and single heads of household units, it is assumed that 85 percent of basic employees are heads of households with families and 15 percent are single; 60 percent of construction and railroad employees are heads of households with families and 40 percent are single; and 40 percent of local service employees are heads of households with families, with the remaining 60 percent single or drawn from families already in the area.

The number of school age children is derived by assuming 1.2 school age child per family unit. This figure divided by 25 students per classroom gives an estimated number of classrooms that would be needed as a result of the new population.

The forecast for housing units needed assumes that demand for permanent site housing would equal 85 percent of mining employees, 90 percent of all other basic employees,

10 percent of construction and railroad employees, and 30 percent of local service employees. Demand for mobile homes would equal 15 percent of mining employees, 10 percent of all other basic employees, 75 percent of construction and railroad employees, and 30 percent of local service employees. (The remaining 40 percent of local service employees, plus the remaining 15 percent of construction and railroad employees, are assumed to be members of a family already in the area, or living with another worker in temporary quarters.)

The above percentages for each of the three employee categories are based on the following assumptions:

1. *The availability of permanent or site housing.** It is assumed more people would move into permanent rental or owner occupied housing if it were made available at the time of their arrival in the area. The figures in this report are based on the assumption that sufficient housing units will be made available to meet the yearly demand. To the extent site housing is *not* provided, the number of campers, trailers, and mobile homes will be increased.

2. *The perception of permanence.* Until the development is perceived to be a continuing industry with the accompanying growth in the area steady and stable, the incoming employees are less likely to demand site housing or bring their families and settle. When the development is acknowledged as permanent, in-migrants are more likely to establish permanent residence. Perception of permanence will also lead some greater number of mobile home residents to shift into site housing.

3. *Construction employees.* A primary consideration in calculating housing and schoolroom demand is that the construction work force tends to be more mobile and workers see themselves as temporary members of the community. There tends to be a higher proportion of single men; many of them bring mobile homes, camper/trailers, or tents with them and commute long distances on weekends. Those who do bring their families tend to live in mobile homes. Therefore, the construction work force creates less demand for permanent site housing and school facilities.

---

*Site housing includes single men boarding houses and single and multi-family dwelling units, both rental and owner occupied.

4. *Basic and local service employees.* It is assumed that these people perceive their work situation as permanent. They move to the area with their families to establish a "home town." To this extent, they expect family type housing, good schools for their children, and urban services and facilities. They probably anticipate rapid integration into community life.

For these reaons, the percent of basic and local service employees having families and desiring housing is higher than for the construction work force. The number of permanent housing units required by these employees is entered as a total figure in the fourth year after arrival. This technique avoids estimating varying portions of the total demand that will be required in each intervening year.

POSSIBLE AREAS FOR INDUSTRY SUPPORT OF LOCAL GOVERNMENT

Two categories of local support are listed:

1. Lobbying or influence in the Wyoming State Legislature or executive agencies to ease Sweetwater County problems.
2. Financial support for public facility construction and public facility or public service operations for which there are not adequate public moneys.

No attempt has been made to rank these. Some are evidently very important and others less so. Such ranking is a matter for local priority setting; until that is done it is pointless to sum the costs of important and unimportant items as if they were comparable.

CATEGORY I TOPICS—LOBBYING

Legislative efforts which may merit industry lobbying efforts include:

1. Assuring the permanence of the new 1 percent local sales tax, a vital component of Green River and Rock Springs municipal budgets.
2. Authorizing strong mobile home safety regulations.
3. Appropriating larger sums to the industrial road fund and raising the ceiling on amounts receivable by a single county to at least $500,000 per year.
4. Clearly permitting local governments to accumulate capital funds from such sources as tap fees.

83

5. Authorizing higher salaries for elected local officials.

6. Orienting public school foundation legislation toward quick response to problems of growth impacted school districts.

7. Supporting authorization of a Wyoming Community Development Agency.

8. At the congressional level, passage of the proposed BLM Organic Act, particularly if amended to duplicate the 1964 Land Sales Act (now inoperative) which would permit municipalities to more easily acquire BLM land for various purposes, including amelioration of housing deficiencies.

CATEGORY II ITEMS—FINANCIAL SUPPORT

Capital construction funds beyond those considered readily available by local government officials are wanted for these projects:

1. *School facilities.* Rock Springs has accumulated an improvements, facilities, and equipment deficit of about $2 million of omitted items (playgrounds, equipment, etc.) as of 1974-75, and prior to completion of buildings to be built under the recently passed bond issue. Funding for the new buildings will also be inadequate and the deficit will increase.

   Green River faces a similar situation with a deficit of over $1 million, including the financially necessary omission of auditorium, football field, etc., from the proposed new high school. The Westerly project near Jamestown will further aggravate the situation unless the developers build and dedicate needed school buildings.

   Both Rock Springs and Green River need more portable classrooms than they can afford (these can be either rented or purchased; a two classroom unit costs about $25,000).*

   Western Wyoming College is seeking $3.5 million for its mock mine and continuum center, oriented toward vocational training and spouse support programs.

---

*The need for such units is dramatized by recent experience at the Reliance school (Rock Springs District) where September 1972 enrollment was 113; September 1973 was 260; and April 1974 was 358.

All of the above school systems have nearly exhausted
their bonding capacity under present state constitutional limitations to complete their building programs in any way.

2. *Municipal facilities.* Rock Springs needs to raise at
least $750,000 for its matching portion of a major
sewage disposal system project within the next three
years. If the present sales tax and the present revenue sharing structure continue, it will be able to
do this with little bonding, although it will require
a large share of available capital funds.

Green River will need to raise $75,000 to $100,000
for its matching share of sewage disposal system ad-
ditions. Rock Springs must acquire many existing
buildings (and land) to rationalize its streets and
traffic flows. This requires several hundred thou-
sand dollars per year, and will be a slow process if
it depends solely on public revenues.

Rock Springs and Green River both need major addi-
tions to streets, roads, and structures (Rock Springs
beltway and Green River overpasses) which will be
slow in completion under present local, state, and
federal funding procedures. Both communities have
extensive unmet needs for recreation facilities (and
programs; see section on services). Since the bond
issue for a Rock Springs recreation facility failed
two years ago, the city has been seeking to put together money to proceed. One possibility would be
industrial contributions on the order of $500,000
(the proposed recreation and park complex capital
cost is estimated at about $1.5 million).

In-town youth centers for both Rock Springs and Green
River would be desirable; no cost estimates are immediately available, but each community would need a
facility costing hundreds of thousands of dollars if
swimming and gymnasium facilities were included.

Green River urgently needs an addition to its city
hall. Rock Springs has plans for (and needs) a $23
million urban renewal project (1972 dollars).

3. *Other facilities.* Housing needs are covered in the
text of this report.

The county hospital to be built in Rock Springs will
probably be underfunded for equipment and furnishings
by $100,000 to $200,000, even if adequate construction money can be raised.

A maxi-clinic (a larger facility with some emergency
room capability) in Green River will require an additional $50,000 to $100,000.

Sweetwater County will soon have to lengthen the airport runway, with a local cost of $200,000. More terminal space will be needed, also.

Child care (day care facilities) are needed. A social club or meeting place is needed for an effective alcoholism control program.

4. *School services.* Both Rock Springs and Green River have put high priorities on hiring and retaining teachers, and have been unable to budget for counseling or school social work personnel to match increased enrollment. Much of the increased enrollment has been made up of children from transient construction families who often present special learning problems; each school district needs several tens of thousands of dollars per year to better maintain educational quality under these circumstances.

5. *Municipal services.* Rock Springs engineering and planning department needs three additional professionals and three maintenance personnel. Green River needs three professionals, in addition to their new administrative assistant, for planning-engineering* (as an alternative to money contributions, industry might consider loaning engineering, administrative, or data processing personnel to local governments for six months to two years).

---

*The town of Green River has no planning staff; Sweetwater County has one planner. Tentative agreement was earlier reached for Green River to contribute about $10,000 to the county for the coming year to augment the County Planning Office with a zoning and building inspector/sanitarian. In turn, a town-county planning operation would be established. This would substantially benefit the county, and particularly, the town, which has many unmet planning and zoning needs. Green River would also be a more active participant in planning for the proposed Westerly development, under that agreement.

Unfortunately, Green River's limited resources precluded making this contribution; a higher priority was given (understandably) to hiring a full-time administrative assistant to the mayor (who is employed full-time elsewhere and has impossible demands made upon his time). The county has gone ahead to hire a sanitarian and an inspector.

However, an industry contribution of $10,000 would still probably put together this arrangement, meeting this Green River and county need. It would also be a valuable indicator of industry concern with long-range problem solving as well as industry availability for crisis response.

86

Substantially more elaborate organized recreation programs are needed; the combined staff and operating costs for Rock Springs and Green River could be $75,000 to $150,000 per year.

6. *Other services.* Health services improvement can probably best be achieved through industry backing of the embryonic health maintenance organization (HMO), Sweetwater Health Services, Inc. The most important backing is encouragement of enrollment in the HMO, but the HMO also needs additional funds for: 1) rotating interns into Sweetwater County, $50,000/year; 2) a revolving fund of $100,000 to $200,000 for facilities construction, including facilities in satellite population centers; and 3) $25,000 to $50,000 for planning an augmentation of health services.

The Southwest Counseling Service (the mental health clinic) could substantially expand its services with an additional $25,000 to $40,000 per year.

STATUS OF LOCAL GOVERNMENT WANTS

This list has been compiled *after* reviewing local government budgets for the 1974-75 fiscal year. Thus, local governments have taken care of some of the needs mentioned in earlier compilations. This is particularly true of wants for vehicles and equipment, and of the need to increase compensation of public employees.

One other point to be made concerns the relevant limitations placed upon local government, by the state constitution, in raising money by bonds for public facilities. A county can bond up to 2 percent of its assessed valuation, a school district up to 10 percent, and a city up to 4 percent (plus 4 percent for sewage disposal systems), all by vote of the people.

The various units of government thus have different constraints on their ability to finance capital improvements. They also have pursued somewhat different policies within these constraints. Sweetwater County has bonded itself for its courthouse and its hospital, and has relatively little bonding capacity left. The school districts are constantly pushing their bonding limits, and are constantly short of facilities. Western Wyoming College is close to its limit. Green River is considering asking the

---

Consideration should also be given to a similar money contribution to the Rock Springs Planning Office; this would let them update their comprehensive plan in appreciably less than the 18 months now scheduled.

voters for bonds for its fire-ambulance garage, for sewage treatment facilities and for city hall expansion. Rock Springs is more hesitant to ask its voters for bonds after the defeat of the recreation facility bond issue two years ago, but will probably require bonds for sewage treatment facilities.

THE RESIDENTS OF
SWEETWATER COUNTY,
WYOMING: A NEEDS
ASSESSMENT SURVEY *

INTRODUCTION

The information on which the present study is based represents the cumulative input of 400 residents of Sweetwater
County. The report synthesizes their perceptions of life
in the county, particularly the problem areas. If the
tone of the report appears to have a negative coloring,
it is because the research effort focused on problem
identification, with the expectation that the results
would be utilized to provide solutions to some of the
county's problems. That emphasis precludes the introduc-
tion of "boosterism" into the process.

BBC wishes to thank those 400 people who participated so
enthusiastically in the study. Their cooperation was se-
cured after assuring them that their answers would point
to solutions to the county's problems. It is our hope
that their opinions will not go unheeded.

---

*Prepared for Denver Research Institute, University
of Denver, as a part of the research project sponsored by
Rocky Mountain Energy Company. The judgments and interp-
retations of this report are considered by the researchers
to be justified by the data, but do not necessarily represent the views of the sponsor. Prepared by Carl von E.
Bickert, Bickert, Browne, Codding & Associates, Inc., 100
South Madison Street, Denver, Colorado 80209, October 1974.

SUMMARY AND CONCLUSIONS

On balance, the negative aspects of day-to-day life for newcomers to Sweetwater County appear to outweight the plus factors. Besides the general friendliness of some of the residents--a character trait not wholly obvious to some recent arrivals--the outdoor pursuits of hunting, fishing, and camping constitute the major charms of the area. Many individuals derive their major enjoyment from the high wage scales and employment opportunities available.

Despite the general feeling that the present boom conditions will persist for many years, there is a perceived "dead-end" quality to much of the employment in the county. Present job satisfaction is relatively high, yet expectations for greater job satisfaction in the future are limited. Also, many individuals--particularly those living in the outlying areas--expect their present employment to terminate within several years.

Although newcomers are more likely to perceive the quality of life in the county as on the upswing, they still give Sweetwater County comparatively lower marks on the provision of key services than former places of residence. Especially poor by comparison are the following services and facilities: 1) medical facilities, 2) parks, 3) housing, and 4) street maintenance and traffic flows. Older residents of the county are more apt to see a deterioration in the local quality of life, primarily due to the negative consequences of rapid growth such as congestion, an increased crime rate, and the influx of undesirable people.

The two major problems are seen as the lack of adequate medical facilities and a shortage of suitable housing. The first is definitely a problem which calls for a fairly immediate solution. Nearly one-third of the citizens of the area go outside the county for routine medical care. A trip to Salt Lake City--nearly 200 miles away--for medical attention is not an uncommon occurrence. Because many of the existing doctors are unable to accept new patients, there is a very real need for more physicians in the county. Also, a larger hospital is called for. The inadequacies of the present medical facilities are especially deplored by newcomers.

Housing, although not as pressing a problem as inadequate medical attention, is regarded as critical to the continued residence of many newcomers. Many recent arrivals in the county experienced difficulty in obtaining suitable housing and have settled for mobile homes, often located in rural areas inconveniently located to the source of key services.

Dissatisfaction with mobile homes as residences was apparent--permanent, single family housing is preferred by a

7 to 1 majority with ownership an important factor. Apartment living has little appeal, primarily due to the lack of privacy. The principal complaint about present housing has to do with a lack of interior space. Whereas the norm in Sweetwater County is two and one-half bedrooms and one bath, the ideal home would consist of three bedrooms and two bathrooms. Landscaping--the provision of trees and lawns--is all important. To obtain such housing individuals are willing to endure a long commute to work--on the average of 14 miles one way. Also, Sweetwater County residents would increase their present housing cost by $50 a month to have the type of home they desire.

Another major problem area--especially in Rock Springs--is traffic flow. The solutions to that problem, however, are easily identifiable--additional stoplights and improvements of existing highways and streets. The problems of congestion and high prices, although regarded as major, do not appear to be amenable to concrete solutions.

Newcomers complain about a shortage of entertainment and recreational facilities. Swimming pools, more bowling alleys, and a recreation center--especially one accessible to children of high school age--are needed. However, adult recreational and socialization needs are also not being met. Women need a place to congregate during the day in a casual atmosphere--without the formal structure imposed by bridge clubs, sewing clubs, the Red Cross, etc. Married couples could use nicer restaurants and clubs where they could go in the evening without the fear of brawling and harassment by unattached males.

Improved retail facilities--especially in Green River--would be a boon to area residents. A major department store, offering a wider clothing selection than presently available, would be welcomed.

There is another problem confronting Sweetwater County--a problem which defies ready solution. That is the general malaise emanating from a number of factors, but principally arising from the lack of real commitment to the future welfare of the community. Personal commitment and interest go hand-in-hand with a position of community establishment; e.g., long time residence, high income, white-collar occupation. On the other hand, alienation--the perception of powerlessness in dealing with one's personal environment--is more apparent among newcomers, low income groups, and individuals with a great deal of previous residential mobility.

That lack of commitment manifests itself in an unwillingness to become involved in community affairs and a disinterest in local politics. Newcomers perceive themselves as too removed from the power structure to change it. Old timers may have sought political involvement in the past,

91

but frustration there and with recent community changes has implanted a "what's the use?" attitude.

One other problem area deserves attention. Sweetwater County is definitely a male environment. Although women engage in the primary recreational pursuits of fishing, hunting, and camping, it is through the instigation of the male. The male emphasis and the lack of recreational and social outlets for women has led to a greater alienation among women than men. The situation is especially acute in the rural areas where women, by their own report, are more dissatisfied with their personal lives and less interested in becoming involved in the community. Female respondents suggest that the presence of a social-recreation center where women could gather during the day to swim, play tennis, bowl, or just chat, would alleviate the situation. Also, a referral service through which women newly arrived in the area could obtain information on key services and facilities in the community would be a welcome addition.

METHODOLOGY

The objectives of the present survey were threefold:

1. To identify those key characteristics of Sweetwater County residents which would aid in community development policy making.

2. To pinpoint the community's problems, and proposed solutions, as perceived by its citizens.

3. To identify those perceptions and attitudes which would assist housing development decisions.

In order to answer those three questions, personal interviews were conducted in 400 randomly selected households in Sweetwater County. A 21-page questionnaire (page 153) was developed and pretested in the county. The interview schedule was designed to maximize respondent interest. In addition to the 400 personal interviews, two focused-group discussions were held with women who had participated in the large scale survey. The 13 women who participated in the group discussions were selected on the basis of their ability to articulate and amplify problems facing the community.

A sample size of 400 households was chosen for two reasons:

1. It would provide results with an error margin no greater than 5 percent at the 95 percent level of confidence.

92

2. The sample would be sufficiently large to permit an analysis by location of residence; i.e., Rock Springs, Green River, and the rural areas. Based on estimates of the total number of households in each of those three locations which were supplied by the Sweetwater County Planning and Zoning Office, the following number of interviews was allocated for each location:

- Rock Springs--198 interviews
- Green River--- 87 interviews
- Rural areas---115 interviews

Each of the two cities was divided into a series of squares on a grid map. Segments were then randomly selected from those grids, and three interviews allocated to each segment. Interviews were provided with a serpentine pattern to follow within each segment, selecting every third household.

The sample of households in the rural areas was selected in a different fashion. Visits were made to each housing location in Sweetwater County (ranging from Granger in the west to Wamsutter in the east) and the number of housing units in each location was recorded. That number included dwelling units on the outskirts of Rock Springs and Green River, but outside the city limits. The total number of estimated housing units was broken up into blocks of four units each and 38 such units selected at random. Interviewers were instructed to obtain three interviews within each unit, following the same type of serpentine pattern as employed in the Rock Springs and Green River sampling procedures.

The overall sampling plan contained one limitation in that model units were not included in the sample. Therefore, the sample may have excluded some short time residents, some of whom may have visited Sweetwater County on a tentative basis and then moved on. In other words, input from the most transient of the short timers may be missing.

All of the interviewers on the survey were members of BBC's interviewing staff who were transported to Sweetwater County from Denver. Those individuals were especially trained in the use of the questionnaire. The interviewing was supervised by a BBC field supervisor, Jack Garvey. All interviewing was conducted between September 9 and 14, 1974. The two focused-group interviews were done on September 23 and 24, 1974.

Upon completion of the interviews, the answers were coded and keypunched on standard IBM cards. Six cards were needed to record the data from each respondent, thus yielding a total of 2,400 IBM cards. The data were tabulated and cross-tabulated, using a CDC 6400 Computer.

Certain factors--such as location and type of residence, occupation, sex, and length of residence in Sweetwater County--were thought to be particularly valuable in analyzing the character of the sample population and identifying subgroups within that population. Every question, therefore, was cross-tabulated by location of residence. In addition, key questions were also cross-tabulated by the other factors. A total of 613 such cross-tabulations were made. However, in order to facilitate the readability of this report, only selected tables are presented throughout its text.*

Table B-I identifies the subgroups formed by each of these major analysis factors.

These subgroup categories are used throughout the report to describe attitudes of the sample population. By identifying attitudes vis-à-vis these subgroups, results become more specific and thus more meaningful.

The interrelationships among these subgroups allow additional specificity and the reader is able to identify clusters within the sample population. The clusters, such as those shown in Tables B-II and B-III, reveal predominant living patterns in the county.

Table B-II gives an overview of the interrelationships among employment, length of residence, and dwelling type subgroups. The clusters which are revealed are: 1) newcomers are predominantly career construction or otherwise employed and live in mobile homes; 2) three to 9.9 year residents are in the minority and have moved into permanent single family housing; 3) long time residents--comprised primarily of other employment and retired categories--are in the majority and obviously prefer and have obtained permanent single family housing.

Table B-III identifies these three factors by location of residence. We have used absolute numbers rather than percentages. In this way the reader may create whatever table of clusters about which he or she may be curious. For instance, Rock Springs residents tend to be long time residents living in permanent single family housing. Also,

---

*In many of the tables in the report, the percentages do not total 100 percent. In those instances in which the columns total less than 100 percent, only the major response categories have been reported. Miscellaneous responses have been excluded in the interests of brevity. In those tables where the responses total to more than 100 percent, this is due to the inclusion of multiple responses.

TABLE B-I

Sample Subgroup Sizes

Subgroup	Number in Sample	Percent of Total
Total sample	400	100%
Location of Residence		
Rock Springs (within city limits)	198	49
Green River (within city limits)	87	22
Rural (anything outside city limits, much of which is within a three-mile fringe radius)	115	29
Sex		
Male	195	49
Female	205	51
Length of Residence in County		
Newcomers (less than three years)	157	39
Medium length of residence (three to 9.9 years)	50	13
Long time residents (10 years and over)	190	48
	N=397	
Type of Residence		
Permanent, single family home dwellers	250	63
Mobile home dwellers	124	31
Apartment, condominium dwellers	24	6
	N=398	
Industry of Employment for Head of Household		
Trona mining and processing	71	20
Career construction	82	24
Other construction	29	8
All other employment categories	165	48
Total employed	347	
Unemployed and retired	50	

TABLE B-II

Clusters of Respondents by Employment and Length of Residence Categories and Distribution of Housing Arrangements for Each Cluster

	Trona mining and Processing Employees	Career Construction Employees	All Other Employee Categories	Retired and Unemployed
Newcomers living in	24	61	68	4
Permanent / Mobile homes	33% / 46%	18% / 77%	35% / 54%	100% / 0%
Medium time residents living in	13	7	29	1
Permanent / Mobile homes	69% / 31%	43% / 57%	72% / 24%	100% / 0%
Long time residents living in	34	14	97	45
Permanent / Mobile homes	82% / 9%	86% / 7%	90% / 7%	93% / 4%

N = 397

Employment, Housing Type, and Length of Residence in County by
Location of Residence

		Trona	Career Construc- tion	All Other Employment Categories	Retired and Unemployed	
ROCK SPRINGS	N/P	1	2	15	2	
	N/MH	0	4	4	0	34 Newcomers
	N/O	0	2	4	0	
	M/P	4	2	16	1	
	M/MH	1	0	1	0	26 Medium length residents
	M/O	0	0	1	0	
	LTR/P	21	11	67	29	
	LTR/MH	1	0	3	0	138 Long time residents
	LTR/O	2	1	2	1	
	Subtotal Employment	30	22	113	33	(N=198)
GREEN RIVER	N/P	6	4	7	1	
	N/MH	8	0	3	0	34 Newcomers
	N/O	4	1	0	0	
	M/P	4	1	5	0	
	M/MH	2	1	1	0	14 Medium length residents
	M/O	0	0	0	0	
	LTR/P	7	1	17	8	
	LTR/MH	0	0	0	2	37 Long time residents
	LTR/O	1	0	1	0	
	Subtotal Employment	32	8	34	11	(N=85)
RURAL	N/P	1	5	2	0	
	N/MH	3	43	30	1	89 Newcomers
	N/O	1	0	3	0	
	M/P	1	0	0	0	
	M/MH	1	3	5	0	10 Medium length residents
	M/O	0	0	0	0	
	LTR/P	0	0	3	5	
	LTR/MH	2	1	4	0	15 Long time residents
	LTR/O	0	0	0	0	
	Subtotal Employment	9	52	47	6	(N=114)
	Total Employment	71	82	194	50	Total N=397

Key: N = Newcomer; M = Medium length residents; LTR = Long time residents; P = Permanent single family dwelling; MH = Mobile home;
O = Other.

the largest number of retirees live in Rock Springs. The
rural areas, on the other hand, are populated primarily by
newcomers working in construction and living in mobile
homes. The population of Green River appears to be equally distributed among newcomers and long time residents and
employment categories, and with a high proportion of permanent single family housing.

The reader may find it helpful to refer to this table
often while reading the report.

THE DEMOGRAPHY OF SWEETWATER COUNTY

MARITAL STATUS

Slightly more than 80 percent of the individuals were married, with 9 percent single, and another 10 percent either
divorced or widowed. Although all three locations had approximately the same percentage of married individuals,
the rural areas had the greatest proportion (13 percent)
of single people.

SIZE OF HOUSEHOLD

The average number of individuals per household was 3.4,
ranging from a high of 3.5 in Rock Springs to 3.2 individuals per household in the rural areas. Roughly one-third
of the households had two inhabitants and over half of the
households had either two or three residents. Over half
of the dwellings contained children, about one-third of
them having children five years or younger. Countywide,
nearly two out of five households had children in school.
However, in the rural areas only 27 percent of the households had children in school.

MOBILITY PATTERNS

The majority of inhabitants of Sweetwater County had lived
in the State of Wyoming 20 years or more. Rock Springs
citizens, in particular, were very likely to be long time
Wyoming residents. On the other hand, 42 percent of the
rural inhabitants were true newcomers, having come to the
state in the last year. In fact, among rural dwellers the
median length of residence in Wyoming was 1.8 years.

Despite the long time average residence in Wyoming, the
median length of residence in Sweetwater county was much
lower--8.3 years. One-fourth of the inhabitants of Sweetwater County had lived there under one year and nearly 40

percent had arrived in the county since the beginning of the boom era three years ago. Rock Springs had been least affected by the recent population boom. Only 18 percent of the citizens of that town had arrived in the last three years and 60 percent had lived there 20 years or more. Green River, on the other hand, has been much more affected by recent growth. Nearly a third of the citizens of Green River had moved there within the last year and 38 percent had arrived in the past three years. The median length of residence in Green River was six and a half years. The rural areas contained the greatest percentage of newcomers; slightly more than half of the inhabitants of the outlying areas had lived in the county under one year. In fact, over three-fourths of the rural inhabitants had been in the area less than three years.

The greater mobility of the rural group was also reflected by the fact that they had averaged two moves in the past five years and 21 percent of the inhabitants of the outlying areas had moved five or more times in that same time period. By comparison, only 11 percent of the Green River citizens and 4 percent of the residents of Rock Springs had moved that often within the last five years.

EDUCATION

Only 15 percent of the inhabitants of the county were college graduates, compared with 28 percent who had not finished high school. The greatest proportion of college graduates was found in Rock Springs (17 percent) and the smallest number (10 percent) in the rural areas.

INCOME

The median income countywide was quite high--$13,209. Only 17 percent made less than $7,500 a year, compared with nearly an identical percentage who had incomes in excess of $20,000 a year.

Green River had the greatest heterogeneity in income levels. Whereas 22 percent of the population of that town had annual incomes less than $7,500, 21 percent had more than $20,000 a year, and better than one out of eight residents of the town had incomes in excess of $25,000. Nevertheless, citizens of Green River had the lowest median income ($12,750), with the median incomes of Rock Springs residents and rural inhabitants nearly identical and slightly higher.

Table B-IV displays the demographic characteristics of Sweetwater County.

TABLE B-IV
Demographic Characteristics

	Total County	Rock Springs	Green River	Rural Areas
Marital Status				
Married	82%	82%	83%	81%
Single	9	7	5	13
Divorced/widowed	10	11	12	5
Mean size of household	3.4	3.5	3.3	3.2
Households with Children				
Have children 5 years or younger	32%	29%	31%	36%
Have children in school	38	42	40	27
Residence and Mobility				
Median number of years in Wyoming	More than 20	More than 20	16.8	1.8
Median number of years in Sweetwater County	8.3	More than 20	6.6	Less than 1
Number of Moves in Past 5 Years				
0	50%	69%	52%	15%
1	16	11	20	21
2-4	20	12	17	37
5 or more	10	4	11	21
Educational Levels				
Did not graduate from high school	28%	25%	26%	34%
High school graduates	73	75	73	66
College graduates	15	17	15	10
Income Levels				
Less than $7,500	17%	16%	22%	15%
$20,000 or more	16	15	21	16
Median income	$13,209	$13,357	$12,750	$13,235

PLACE OF EMPLOYMENT

The two major employment categories in Sweetwater County
(Table B-V) were construction (27 percent of all heads of
households) and trona mining (18 percent).* Of the construction workers, 74 percent considered themselves to be
career construction employees and 15 percent of the total
work force are employed in building the Jim Bridger plant.

The heavy emphasis on mining or construction work was
least in Rock Springs, where 17 percent of the individuals were employed in construction and 15 percent in mining.
In Green River, the miners (37 percent) outnumbered the
construction workers (12 percent) by about three to one.
In the rural areas, 59 percent of the individuals were employed in construction and 8 percent in trona mining.

About half of the newcomers to the county were employed in
construction and 15 percent in mining.

TABLE B-V

Occupation and Place of Employment of Head of Household

	Total County	Rock Springs	Green River	Rural Areas
Employed in trona mining and processing	18%	15%	37%	8%
Career construction worker employed at Jim Bridger plant	12	5	5	30
Other career construction worker	8	7	3	15
Other construction worker	8	5	4	14
Retired	12	14	14	4
Unemployed	2	3	1	1
Other employment categories	28	36	28	19
Self-employed	3	2	2	4
Engineers	3	5	0	4
Teachers	3	3	5	1
Managers and administrators	3	5	1	0
Total N = 400	100%	100%	100%	100%

*These percentages are based on the total sample of
400 respondents; the percentages (32 percent construction,
20 percent mining) in Table B-I are based on the actual
number of employed respondents.

101

The average length of time the individuals had been employed in their present job was slightly less than two
years, countywide (Table B-VI). Job longevity was highest
in Rock Springs (median length = 4.0 years), slightly less
in Green River (median length = 3.5 years), and least in
the rural areas--where the median length of employment had
been eight and one-half months.

TABLE B-VI

Length of Employment

	Total County	Rock Springs	Green River	Rural Areas
Length of Time in Present Job				
One year or less	32%	18%	27%	60%
1-5 years	21	25	15	20
Over 5 years	28	35	36	11
No answer	19	22	22	9
Median length in years	1.9	4.0	3.5	0.7
Anticipated Length of Employment in Present Job				
One year or less	14%	7%	11%	30%
1-5 years	24	19	16	38
Over 5 years	38	44	51	20
Don't know	3	4	0	3
No answer	21	26	22	9
Median length in years	5.0	More than 5	More than 5	1.9

Over half of the residents of the county had occupational
skills other than those presently being utilized. However,
two-thirds of the newcomers had other occupational skills.
Those presently non-utilized skills ranged from that of
construction craftsman (a skill found primarily in Rock
Springs and Green River) to that of an operative. Also
present were mechanics and repairmen, carpenters, and all
types of professional workers.

One-fourth of the women interviewed were employed, with
female employment highest in Rock Springs (29 percent) and
lowest in the rural areas (20 percent). The major female
occupational category was clerical (11 percent); 4 percent
classified themselves as private household workers; and 3
percent taught in public schools. Only 2 percent were employed as retail sales personnel. Nearly all of the employed women in Rock Springs worked in the city, whereas

only half of the employed women in Green River worked in
that community. Four percent were employed at the Jim
Bridger plant. Employed women living in the outlying
areas were likely to be working at any number of locations,
including Rock Springs (7 percent), the Jim Bridger plant
(4 percent), Green River (3 percent), and Superior (3 percent).

Slightly more than one-third of the women indicated that
they had occupational skills which were not being utilized
at the present. Those skills were generally clerical or
as food service workers.

For most men in Sweetwater County, the average commuting
time to work was slightly in excess of one-half hour. Men
in Rock Springs had the easiest time of it--a commute of
slightly less than 20 minutes. However, working men in
Green River and the outlying areas took close to 35 minutes to get to work. For the average woman who was employed in Sweetwater County, the commute to work was
likely to involve about a 10 minute drive.

EVALUATION OF EMPLOYMENT OPPORTUNITIES IN SWEETWATER COUNTY

Nearly 40 percent of the individuals felt that they were
doing better financially in Sweetwater County than they
could do anywhere else. Another 35 percent were of the
opinion that their financial opportunities were as good
locally as could be found. Only 10 percent stated that
they could do better financially in another location.
That feeling of being able to better oneself financially
elsewhere was strongest in Rock Springs and least among
rural inhabitants, nearly half of whom regarded themselves
as having excellent financial opportunities in the county.

The opportunity for financial gain was certainly not lost
on newcomers, 50 percent of whom indicated that they were
doing better in Sweetwater County than they could do anywhere else. Career construction employees also were of
the opinion that they were doing as well or better than
they could in another location. Miners were not as im-
pressed with their ability to improve themselves financially in Sweetwater County, but were certainly of the opinion
that they were doing as well financially in that location
as they might anywhere else.

Approximately three-fourths of the inhabitants indicated
that their opportunities to get ahead in ther career and
the chance to take advantage of their skills and abilities
were as good or better in Sweetwater County than elsewhere.

The average individual in Sweetwater County expected his present job to last for another five years (see Table B-VI). The job expectations were longer than that in Rock Springs and Green River, but less than two years in the rural areas. Newcomers had an average job expectancy of 2.7 years, with 30 percent anticipating that their jobs would last more than five years and a similar percentage expecting them to terminate within a year.

Miners had employment expectancies in excess of five years. However, career construction workers predicted their present employment to last on the average of 2.4 years. Nearly one-fourth of the construction workers indicated that their present job would probably end within one year.

In most instances--particularly among rural inhabitants-- the termination of employment will coincide with job completion (e.g., completion of construction of the Jim Bridger plant). Nearly one-fourth of the workers expected to retire in their present positions. That figure reached slightly more than one-third in Rock Springs. However, only 7 percent of the rural residents expected to retire in their present jobs. On the other hand, 12 percent of the workers living in the outlying areas expected to move on to another job which would be more attractive than their present employment. Another 11 percent in the same residence category anticipated being transferred by their present employer to another location.

If construction activity in Sweetwater County were to slack off--resulting in a layoff for the head of the household--over half (57 percent) of the career construction workers would seek construction employment in some other location. Another 18 percent would search for other types of employment in some other location than Sweetwater County. Only 10 percent of the career construction workers would look for local employment, if it were available.

However, few individuals predicted the present boom in mining and construction to tail off in less than ten years. Only 8 percent expected the boom to die out in less than five years. If such an event occurred (i.e., a leveling off of present mining and construction activities), 36 percent of the residents would expect to leave Sweetwater County (Table B-VII). The exodus would be greatest in the outlying areas, where two-thirds of the residents would expect to leave. However, even if the boom continued, 30 percent of the residents countywide would expect to leave. Under those circumstances the greatest stability could be expected in Green River. The continuation of the boom would have the least impact in Rock Springs, where roughly 24 percent of the residents anticipate leaving, boom or no

104

TABLE B-VII

Expectations for Leaving the Area

	Total County	Rock Springs	Green River	Rural Areas
Expect to leave the area if the boom continues	30%	25%	17%	47%
Expect to leave the area if the boom dies out	36	23	22	66

boom. The greatest difference would be felt in the rural areas where, if the boom were to continue, 47 percent would leave. However, if it were to end, two-thirds of the rural inhabitants would expect to leave the county.

No single reason would account for an exodus under continued boom conditions. The major reason for leaving--particularly among rural inhabitants--had to do with a general dislike of the area. Other reasons for leaving included 1) congestion and overcrowding (particularly anathema to Rock Springs and Green River citizens), 2) a return to a prior place of residence (anticipated more by rural inhabitants), and 3) a transfer by the present employer (again mentioned more frequently by rural residents).

PROBLEM AREAS AND PRIORITIES

The identification of perceived problem areas and their impact on the residents of the county was handled in several ways. First, respondents were merely asked to identify the three major problems confronting the county and then to discuss possible solutions. This type of "free response" approach enables the researcher to work within the respondent's framework, even though that framework may be highly idiosyncratic.

Another approach entailed asking respondents to give their impressions of the direction in which the local community is moving. Such movement--when it occurs--is perceptible and has been monitored in urban areas undergoing either positive growth or noticeable decline. Since such evaluation involves a non-static condition, the most meaningful estimates are usually obtained from residents with a sufficient sense of history to observe such trends. Newcomers can only report hearsay impressions.

In order to establish some *relative* sense of urgency and
importance to various problem areas, respondents in the
present study were then asked to evaluate the adequacy of
13 community services and facilities, all of which would
exacerbate various community problems. Those services
were examined in several different ways; e.g., their relative importance, the need for improvement before the community would be the kind of place in which one would want
to establish permanent residence, and their costs.

For those individuals who had lived in areas other than
Sweetwater County and thus had a yardstick by which to
evaluate the provision of key services in the county, 19
service areas were rated and compared. For those areas
which were judged to be below standard, suggestions for
improvement were elicited.

Hopefully, the various techniques described above have
provided a comprehensive picture of the local problems and
priorities as perceived by the inhabitants of Sweetwater
County.

MAJOR PROBLEM AREAS

Countywide, by far the biggest perceived problem was inadequate housing (45 percent), receiving more than twice
as many mentions as did the second most pressing concern.
Following in order were these problems:

1. Poor traffic flows (27 percent).

2. Inadequate medical facilities and shortage of medical
    personnel (15 percent).

3. Congestion and overcrowded conditions (20 percent).

4. High prices and cost of living (20 percent).

5. Lack of paved streets and roads (19 percent).

6. Poor or overcrowded public school facilities (17 per-
    cent).

7. Lack of entertainment and recreational facilities
    (including for young people)(23 percent).

8. Crime and drugs (13 percent).

9. Poor sewage disposal (11 percent).

10. Inadequate shopping facilities and services (12 per-
    cent).

    1. *Location of residence*. The housing shortage was
viewed as more critical in Green River (62 percent) than
in either of the other two locations, although inadequate
housing was still seen as the major problem in both Rock

106

Springs and the rural areas. Problems related to traffic flows were critical in Rock Springs (39 percent), where they received two to three times the emphasis as in Green River and outlying areas. Congestion and overcrowded conditions were particularly aggravating in Rock Springs and Green River, and much less so in the rural areas (10 percent). High prices received comment from individuals in all three locations. Poorly paved streets and roads were mentioned most often by rural inhabitants and much less frequently by individuals living in Green River.

Criticisms of the school systems were focused in the two cities, rather than in the outlying areas. The shortage of entertainment and recreational facilities was mentioned fairly uniformly throughout the county. The problem of crime and drugs, on the other hand, was regarded as more serious in Rock Springs than elsewhere. The need for better shopping facilities was primarily a Green River problem (21 percent). One other problem which seemed to be particularly indigenous to Green River was the shortage of adequate medical facilities and personnel, mentioned by 31 percent of the residents of that city.

Table B-VIII shows the ranking of the eight problem areas receiving the highest mention on Question 7 of the questionnaire.

2. *Newcomers*. The problem areas especially annoying to newcomers were as follows:

1. Inadequate housing (49 percent).

2. High prices (23 percent).

3. Shortage of entertainment (20 percent).

4. Poorly paved roads and streets (20 percent).

5. Dirt and dust (15 percent).

6. Inadequate shopping facilities (14 percent).

7. Congestion and overcrowded conditions (12 percent).

8. Poor traffic flows (12 percent).

Therefore, newcomers were more concerned than were the long time residents about housing, lack of entertainment and recreational facilities, high prices, dirt and dust, and poor shopping facilities. On the other hand, recent arrivals were much less concerned about congestion (probably because they had never seen the area otherwise), poor schools, sewage disposal, poor traffic enforcement, and problems related to crime and drugs.

3. *Expected length of residence in the area*. Those individuals who anticipated leaving the area within a year

TABLE B-VIII

Major Problem Areas by Location of Residence

Rock Springs		Green River		Rural	
Poor traffic flows	39%	Inadequate housing	62%	Inadequate housing	44%
Inadequate housing	38	Medical facilities and shortage of personnel	31	Lack of paved streets and roads	25
Lack of entertainment and recreational facilities	26	High prices and cost of living	24	High prices and cost of living	19
Congestion and overcrowded conditions	25	Congestion and overcrowded conditions	23	Lack of entertainment and recreation facilities	19
Poor or overcrowded public school facilities	21	Inadequate shopping facilities and services	21	Poor water quality and/or facilities	17
Lack of paved streets and roads	19	Lack of entertainment and recreational facilities	19	Poor traffic flows	17
High prices and cost of living	18	Poor or overcrowded public school facilities	17	Dust and dirt	13
Crime and drugs	17	Poor traffic flows	14	Poor sewage disposal	13

were much less concerned about housing shortages than were
individuals who may be here as long as five years. In
other words, poor housing conditions are tolerable for
relatively short periods of time. Nor were transients as
concerned with the congestion problem as were people who
expect to live in the area the rest of their lives. The
very "short-timers" saw two very immediate problems: 1)
the inadequacy of present local medical facilities and 2)
the high cost of living.

   4. *Prior mobility.* The highly mobile Rock Springs
group--although troubled by the lack of housing--was more
concerned about the lack of recreational and entertainment
facilities and the dirt and dust than were the individuals
with prior patterns of residential stability. Also, the
high cost of living was seen as a major problem by the
more mobile individuals. Long time residents of Rock
Springs, however, evidenced more concern about traffic
flows, the poor schools, and crime and drugs than was
voiced by the mobile group.

The very mobile group in Green River also expressed dissatisfaction with present housing conditions and--more
than the individuals who had not moved around a great
deal--complained about the shortage of entertainment and
recreational facilities, poorly paved roads and streets,
and inadequate medical facilities. Residents with long
time roots in Green River evidenced much more concern
about the shortage of medical personnel and facilities,
the poor schools, inconsistent traffic enforcement, and
problems related to crime and drugs.

The most mobile segment of this population subgroup, con-
sisting of residents of the outlying areas, showed a
great deal of concern over housing shortages (52 percent),
the lack of paved streets and roads (30 percent), and the
high cost of living (24 percent).

   5. *Type of prior environment.* At one point in the
interview, respondents with a history of some mobility in
the past 10 years were asked to indicate the type of city
or town in which they had most enjoyed living. On the
basis of their answers, respondents were then categorized
into three types: 1) former large city inhabitants, 2)
ex-small city dwellers, and 3) former small town (or rural)
residents.

Former big city inhabitants now living in Rock Springs
were particularly concerned about inadequate housing (54
percent), the shortage of entertainment and recreational
facilities (38 percent), poor streets and roads (29 percent), congestion and overcrowding (29 percent), and the
lack of better shopping facilities (21 percent). They
were much less concerned with the high prices in the county than were individuals who had formerly lived in small

towns. Former residents of small towns were particularly
perturbed by the inadequate housing (54 percent), poor
traffic planning (32 percent), congestion (29 percent),
and the high prices (25 percent). They showed no concern
over the lack of recreational facilities for young people
in the area--a factor of some importance to both small and
large city dwellers.

Ex-residents of large cities living in Green River were
especially upset by the inadequate housing (56 percent)
and the shortage of shopping facilities (31 percent).
Former small town residents mentioned housing problems (71
percent), high living costs (32 percent), and the shortage
of shopping facilities (21 percent).

Those individuals presently residing in rural areas who
had lived at some previous time in a large city were upset
with the housing shortages (57 percent). More than other
types of residents, they were concerned about the lack of
adequate shopping facilities (19 percent), problems with
traffic flows (19 percent), and poor schools (16 percent).
Only one-third of the former small town residents complained about inadequate housing. In fact, their complaints were much more likely to vary over a large number
of subject areas, with few specific criticisms.

6. *Perceived direction of quality of life in the
area.* Those problems which seem to differentiate between
the people who saw the quality of life in Sweetwater County declining and those who perceived it on the upswing
were as follows (i.e., individuals who saw things in a
more negative light were distressed with the following
problems):

1. Overcrowded conditions.

2. Crime and drugs.

3. Schools.

7. *Present type of dwelling.* Although permanent
home dwellers and mobile home residents had the same overall concerns, the perceived relative seriousness of those
problems varied. For example, permanent homeowners gave
much more weight to the problems of congestion, crime and
drugs, traffic flows, and poor schools. Trailer dwellers,
on the other hand, were more concerned with the dirt and
dust, inadequate housing, and the lack of paved streets.

8. *Employment classification.* The trona miners in
Rock Springs complained of housing shortages (38 percent),
unsatisfactory traffic flows (35 percent), and poor paved
roads and streets (25 percent). Career construction workers in Rock Springs were much more concerned about the
housing shortages (59 percent) and the high cost of living
(36 percent). Also, a number of career construction

110

workers in town complained that the business community was generally uncooperative.

The principal problems perceived by trona miners in Green River were the housing shortage (51 percent) and the high cost of living (33 percent).

Among career construction employees living in the outlying areas, the major problems were housing (44 percent), high living costs (27 percent), and the lack of paved streets and roads (21 percent). Also, the excessive dirt and dust in the outlying areas was a major source of concern to the career construction employees living there.

9. *Income levels.* Generally, the poor school facilities were the concern of the upper income group, whereas the high cost of living in the area was more often mentioned by low income individuals. Housing was a major problem at all income levels, particularly among the most affluent individuals in the outlying areas.

10. *Sex.* The way in which men and women perceived the major problems in the area did not differ to a major degree. Men placed somewhat more importance on the housing problem, traffic enforcement, the shortage of entertainment and recreational facilities, and poor sewage disposal. Women, on the other hand, were likely to be more upset with problems in the educational system, inadequate shopping facilities, and the dirt and dust.

PERCEIVED SOLUTIONS TO MAJOR PROBLEMS

1. *The housing shortage.* Obviously, the major solution to the housing shortage would be to provide more home at all income levels--mentioned by 45 percent of the residents. Another 12 percent indicated that the situation could be alleviated by lower rents and rent ceilings. Another suggestion--mentioned by 10 percent of the residents of the area--would be to release more land presently held by large organizations and make it available for additional housing. Other recommendations included improving the trailer courts (7 percent), leasing trailers and making more mobile homes available (6 percent), company subsidies for employee housing (6 percent), and building more inexpensive homes (6 percent). Five percent of the individuals in the county advocated getting rid of the mobile homes now dotting the landscape.

2. *Traffic flows.* The principal solution to traffic problems was seen as the provision of more stoplights (43 percent). Another 25 percent of the individuals who regarded traffic as a problem would advocate improving the present overpass, belt-loop, and highway system, while another 21 percent recommended widening the streets and

building new ones. One out of 10 individuals who considered traffic flows to be a problem thought that it would
help the situation to straighten out or to blacktop the
present roads. In addition, some of the problems could be
solved with a larger police force (7 percent).

3. *Congestion and overcrowding*. This was one of the
more puzzling problems to solve. For example, one in six
individuals was of the opinion that no solution was possible at this time. On the other hand, 11 percent of the
individuals advocated limiting the population in some
manner, while 10 percent would build more housing to accommodate the growth. Nine percent cited the need for
planning ahead for the future. Many of the other suggested solutions were tangential and scattered--indicating
general confusion about solving this growth problem.

4. *High cost of living*. Like the national economy,
no one appeared to have the answer to the high prices in
Sweetwater County. One out of seven residents gloomily
foresaw no possible solution. Thirteen percent advocated
the establishment of price ceilings and regulations, and
a similar percentage recommended unrestricted competition,
which they thought would drive prices down. Other suggested solutions included general price reductions (9 percent), the provision of more housing (6 percent), the institution of policies by local businesses which would elim-
inate taking advantage of the local consumer (5 percent),
and working with a local merchants association for lower
prices (3 percent).

5. *Paved roads and streets*. Solutions in this area
were much easier to conceptualize. Over half of the individuals who mentioned this as a problem advocated black-
topping, paving, or straightening the present streets.
Another 28 percent indicated that the present streets
should be widened or that new ones should be built. Thirteen percent recommended more stoplights and a similar
percentage advocated the improvement of the present highway system by constructing an overpass or completing the
present belt-loop.

DIRECTION IN WHICH THE COMMUNITY IS SEEN AS MOVING

There was a fairly even split between those people who
perceived the local area as improving and those who saw it
going downhill--with roughly 37 percent of the county in
each of those categories. The other one-fourth of the
population felt that the area has remained fairly stable.
The greatest decline was seen in Rock Springs, where approximately half of the residents of that city were of the
opinion that the quality of life in the community has been
deteriorating, while only 26 percent have witnessed

improvement. In Green River, a slightly larger percentage
viewed the community as moving in a positive direction
versus a negative one. There was the least gloom exhibited in the rural areas. In those locations nearly half
(46 percent) of the residents perceived an upward trend,
with only 16 percent viewing things with a negative per-
spective.

The more positive outlook in the rural areas was undoubt-
edly due to the large concentration of newcomers there.
For example, in the county overall 43 percent of the newcomers viewed the quality of life as being on the upswing,
with only 20 percent taking a negative slant. Among old
timers (i.e., individuals who had lived in the area more
than ten years), the finding was reversed. Among the latter individuals, 48 percent saw life as moving downhill,
with 29 percent perceiving an improvement.

TABLE B-IX

Direction Community is Moving

	Total County	Rock Springs	Green River	Rural Areas	Countywide	
					New-comers	Old-timers
Community thought to be improving	36%	26%	42%	46%	43%	29%
Community thought to be the same	7	9	1	5	5	9
Community thought to be the same (positive)	13	10	17	16	19	10
Community thought to be the same (negative)	5	4	1	9	5	4
Community thought to be going downhill	37	49	37	16	20	48

The major culprits behind the overall perceived decline in
the area were seen as 1) rapid growth, 2) an increase in
crime and general laxity in moral standards, 3) an influx
of undesirable people, and 4) the growth requirements far
outstripping the provision of services.

In Rock Springs the problem of congestion and rapid growth
was regarded as a secondary factor to the increase in
crime, in terms of the factors responsible for the decline
of the area. In addition to the four major causes noted
above, Rock Springs residents were of the opinion that increases in traffic had led to a decline in the quality of

life. In Green River, growth and congestion were viewed
as major contributors to the decline in the quality of
life. Secondary factors included the lagging behind of
key services and an influx of undesirable individuals.
Crime was viewed as less of a causative factor in Green
River than in Rock Springs. The rural areas contained too
few old timers to pinpoint reliably the reasons underlying
the perceived decline of the area.

MOST REWARDING ASPECTS OF LIFE IN THE AREA

Respondents were asked to identify the rewarding aspects
of the local environment. Opinions regarding the positive
aspects of Sweetwater County were varied. No single factor predominated. For example, 18 percent praised the
friendly people in the area; 13 percent indicated that
they enjoyed hunting; a similar percentage mentioned the
enjoyment of fishing; 12 percent cited the neighborhood
or community; and 11 percent were attracted by the total
outdoor recreation scene. Other positive aspects of the
area included the climate and clean air, the open space,
the attractive countryside, the good employment opportunities, the salaries, and overall job satisfaction.

　　　1. *Location of residence.* The friendly people were
most often singled out in the towns of Rock Springs and
Green River (21 percent in each location). Also, the residents of those two towns praised their neighborhoods and
communities, in general. Green River residents found an
added dimension of small town life which they regarded as
extremely relaxing and comfortable.

Inhabitants of the outlying areas found similar rewards in
the area, but in slightly different order. The most positive aspect of local life for the rural inhabitants was
hunting (16 percent). Those individuals also placed high
priority on the good salaries they were enjoying (13 percent). The fishing opportunities were mentioned by 12
percent of the rural residents, who also cited open space
and the friendly people. However, the friendliness factor
was not as apparent to rural inhabitants as it was to residents of the two major towns. Also, individuals in the
outlying areas were most likely (12 percent) to find
nothing good to say about local life.

　　　2. *Newcomers.* The positive factors of the area as
perceived by newcomers were quite similar to those ob-
served by rural residents. In fact, seven rewarding aspects of local life were all mentioned with nearly equal
frequency by newcomers. Those seven factors were:

1. Good salaries.

2. Good employment opportunities.

3. Hunting.

4. Fishing.

5. Outdoor recreation in general.

6. Friendly people.

7. Overall job satisfaction.

Individuals who planned to leave the area within a short
period of time found very little in the way of friendliness to commend it. Individuals with short residency expectations were attracted by the outdoor recreation opportunities but were the most likely to find no reward in
living in Sweetwater County. Also, that same group of individuals did not find their present overall job satisfaction or their salary level as attractive as did the people
who planned to remain in the county longer.

   3. *Income levels*. Both the lowest and highest income groups in Rock Springs contained the highest proportion of individuals who perceived few rewarding aspects to
life in the area. The lower income group was more likely
to mention hunting as an enjoyable pursuit than was the
most affluent group. Also, high income individuals in
Rock Springs were much more likely to perceive the local
inhabitants as friendly than were individuals in the lower
income categories. However, the latter individuals had a
greater tendency to cite their neighborhoods as being enjoyable aspects of local life. Employment opportunities
were often mentioned by the higher income groups in Rock
Springs.

There was less overall dissatisfaction with life in the
area expressed by Green River inhabitants than by individuals who lived in the other two locations. Also, in the
town of Green River, there appeared to be no consistent
relationship between income levels and perceived rewards
of the area.

In the outlying areas, the level of dissatisfaction with
life in general was higher--particularly among the more
affluent, 22 percent of whom were unable to name a rewarding aspect of life in the county. Their rewards were
definitely job-related, with nearly 40 percent of the
highest income group mentioning either the good employment
opportunity or the excellent salary.

   4. *Sex*. There was a great deal of variation between
men and women in terms of the perceived rewards of living
in Sweetwater County. For example, the positive aspects
of hunting, fishing, and outdoor sports in general were
primarily male pursuits and were mentioned by relatively
small percentages of women. Women, on the other hand, experienced greater rewards from the friendly people in the

115

area and the generally relaxed atmosphere. Men were slightly more likely to mention positive employment aspects such as salary, job satisfaction, etc., than were women.

One point certainly deserves mention. Women, in general, were much less satisfied with life in the area. That is, they were much more likely to find nothing positive about living in Sweetwater County. Also, a slightly higher proportion of women than men gave negative remarks when asked to identify the most rewarding aspects of local life.

EVALUATION OF THE IMPORTANCE OF SPECIFIC COMMUNITY SERVICES

Respondents were presented with a list of 13 community services or facilities which, when missing or deficient, are likely to become problem areas. Several techniques were used to assess the importance of those 13 service areas. In one task, individuals were asked to rank the top five and also the bottom three, in terms of the perceived importance of those factors in making the community the kind of place in which the respondent would want to live. A second activity involved indicating which areas would need improvement before the respondent would consider remaining in the community. The third task required the respondent to indicate the five most costly problem areas to solve.

The perceived order of priority for the improvement of existing services was as follows:

1. Medical and mental health services (86 percent).

2. Road and street maintenance (62 percent).

3. Suitable housing (49 percent).

4. Police protection (46 percent).

5. More and better schools and teachers (44 percent).

6. Sanitation services (sewer, garbage collection, etc.) (43 percent).

7. Community planning (36 percent).

8. Retail stores (30 percent).

9. Parks (26 percent).

10. Other recreational facilities such as theaters, bowling alleys, tennis courts, etc. (22 percent).

11. Fire protection (20 percent).

12. Outdoor recreation (19 percent).

13. Availability of favorite television programs (5 percent).

There was no question but that improved medical services was the number one priority, being mentioned as one of the top five problem areas by 86 percent of the residents countywide. Only 2 percent saw it as an area of minor concern. Also, a majority of residents indicated that present medical facilities needed to be improved before they would consider remaining in the area.*

Consistently highly ranked, but lacking the real immediacy connected with the shortage of adequate medical facilities, was the problem of street and road maintenance. Although nearly two-thirds of the residents rated that problem area among the top five, only 29 percent indicated that a solution had to be found before they would consider remaining in the community.

Following closely after street maintenance was the problem of inadequate housing facilities. Nearly half of the individuals rated this problem among the top five, and one-third stated that it would have to be corrected before they would remain in the area.

Schools and sanitation services were viewed with about equal importance--both in terms of overall ratings and the need for improvement before the community would be the kind of place in which the individual would want to remain.

Consistently at the lowest end of the priority scale were outdoor recreation and television programming. Television programming was listed in the first five most pressing problems by only 5 percent of the sample, although 7

---

*At first glance it would appear that there is some discrepancy between the priorities obtained by the present method and the problems identified in the free response situation. For example, in the latter situation, "inadequacy of medical service" was only the seventh ranked problem (mentioned by 15 percent of the residents of the county), whereas it was far-and-away the top priority item in need of solution. However, there is a rational explanation for such a seeming disparity.

Medical problems--which occur infrequently--may not as readily come to mind in a free response situation as the day-to-day nagging problem of poor housing conditions. However, when recall is assisted through the presentation of a list of service areas, an item such as medical service is quite naturally frequently selected. Also, due to their obvious importance, the improvement of inadequate medical services might be taken for granted. In other words, it may be difficult for many people to imagine the continuation of a medically deprived environment, whereas housing problems could continue indefinitely.

percent indicated it would have to be improved before they would consider remaining in the area. However, as Table B-X indicates, this dissatisfaction arises primarily in the rural areas.

The perceived cost of solving various problem areas roughly paralleled their stated priority. The most costly problem to solve was viewed as street maintenance, closely followed by the provision of adequate medical facilities. Those areas were included among the five most costly areas ranked as follows in terms of perceived costs:

3. Better school facilities.

4. Sanitation services.

5. Police protection.

6. Suitable housing.

7. Fire protection.

8. Parks.

9. Other recreational facilities.

10. Community planning.

11. Outdoor recreation.

12. Retail stores.

13. Availability of television.

The problem areas in which the priorities clearly outranked the cost of solution were retail facilities, housing, and community planning. In other words, the perceived costs of solving those problem areas would be disproportionately low when weighed against the importance of their solution.

1. *Location of residence*. As one would imagine, the perceived priority of problems differed markedly from location to location, with one exception; i.e., in all three locations medical services received the top priority ranking. If one looks only at the second measure of priority estimation used—wherein solutions must be provided before the individual would remain in the community—the outlying areas were most critical in terms of the need for problem solution. For example, in those locations, an average of 30 percent of the residents would not consider remaining unless the major problems received fairly immediate solution. In Green River, on the other hand, only 14 percent indicated—on the average—that their continued stay in Green River was contingent upon solution of the major problems. Rock Springs falls between those two extremes, with 22 percent of the residents indicating that their continued stay in the community depended on correction of the major, existing problems.

118

TABLE B-X

Priorities for Problem Solution

Rock Springs			Green River			Rural		
Problem Area	Ranking Item in Top Five Priorities	Would Leave If Service Not Improved	Problem Area	Ranking Item in Top Five Priorities	Would Leave If Service Not Improved	Problem Area	Ranking Item in Top Five Priorities	Would Leave If Service Not Improved
Medical and mental health services	84%	46%	Medical and mental health services	91%	43%	Medical and mental health services	80%	61%
Road and street maintenance	63	27	Road and street maintenance	61	20	Suitable housing	60	45
Local police protection	57	29	Retail stores	55	19	Road and street maintenance	60	39
Local sanitation services	50	28	Suitable housing	53	30	More and better schools and teachers	47	32
More and better schools and teachers	44	26	More and better schools and teachers	41	16	Local sanitation services	37	43
Community planning	42	21	Local police protection	39	5	Local police protection	36	23
Suitable housing	38	26	Community planning	32	13	Retail stores	30	27
Parks	30	16	Local fire protection	30	1	Community planning	26	25
Other recreational facilities	21	19	Local sanitation services	28	13	Other recreational facilities	25	24
Retail stores	19	17	Parks	20	4	Parks	25	15
Outdoor recreation	19	15	Other recreational facilities	19	9	Local fire protection	20	24
Local fire protection	19	15	Outdoor recreation	12	6	Outdoor recreation	20	22
Availability of TV programs	5	5	Availability of TV programs	4	0	Availability of TV programs	10	16

119

Table B-X gives the perceived order of problem-solving priority for each location (Question 14 on questionnaire) juxtaposed against the percent of respondents who would consider leaving Sweetwater County if the problem was not adequately solved soon (Question 14a on questionnaire).

Not only do the priorities differ among three locations, but also the relative degree of seriousness each of the areas attaches to the problems varies. For instance, rural respondents rank improvement of local sanitation services fifth, yet 43 percent of those respondents indicate they will leave if a solution is not forthcoming. Rock Springs residents apparently feel the same way about improving recreational facilities. Green River residents, on the other hand, seemingly demonstrate the greatest degree of willingness to remain in the community despite the problems.

    2. *Newcomers.* Newcomers gave medical services top priority, and slightly more than 60 percent of them indicated that they would not remain in the community unless adequate medical services were provided. Housing was another very key problem area among newcomers, over half of whom indicated that they would not remain unless the problem was solved. The third most important priority area among newcomers was the condition of the roads and streets. Other top ranked areas of major concern were sanitation services, schools, and retail stores. In the latter category, nearly one-third of the newcomers indicated that they would not remain unless there were improved retail facilities.

As Table B-XI illustrates, newcomers were also extremely sensitive to problem solutions, in that approximately 30 percent of them would not consider remaining unless major problems are solved. Even in the lowest rated problem area--the provision of television programming--13 percent of the newcomers said that they would probably not remain unless improved programming were available.

    3. *Sex.* The major differences in perception between men and women occurred in the areas of street maintenance, sanitation services, schools, and housing. Women were much more sensitive to problems in the schools, whereas men expressed greater concern over streets, sanitation, and housing. Men and women alike deplored the present inadequate medical services.

120

TABLE B-XI

Priority of Services--Newcomers

	Ranking Item in Top Five Priorities	Ranking in Bottom Three Priorities	Would Leave If Service Not Improved
Retail stores	38%	29%	31%
Medical and mental health services	82	2	60
Suitable housing for your family's needs	61	4	51
More and better schools and teachers	42	14	31
Road and street maintenance	59	6	35
Local police protection	32	14	22
Local fire protection	17	11	21
Local sanitation services (sewer, garbage collection)	30	14	36
Community planning	32	11	27
Parks	23	24	13[a]
Availability of TV programs you like to watch	6	63	13[a]
Outdoor recreation	18	39	18
Other recreational facilities such as theaters, bowling alleys, tennis courts, etc.	28	33	22

N = 157

[a]This may indicate a core of residents who will leave the area regardless of what improvements are made. Additionally, primarily rural residents indicated dissatisfaction with TV programming; this may be because they are unable to receive cable.

COMPARISON OF SERVICES OFFERED IN SWEETWATER COUNTY WITH THOSE OFFERED ELSEWHERE IN THE COUNTRY

Individuals who had moved to Sweetwater County within the past ten years or so were asked to compare the various services offered locally with those services provided in a former place of residence where they especially enjoyed living. Of the individuals who had come to Sweetwater County in the past decade (i.e., 57 percent), one-third of them mentioned large cities as being a particularly enjoyable place of residence; 28 percent named a small town; 26 percent a small city; and only 6 percent listed a rural

121

setting. Even a substantial proportion of present rural
residents of Sweetwater County (36 percent) mentioned a
location which they categorized as a large city. The average length of time spent in each of those locations
named was more than five years, so that the respondents
should have had an excellent basis for comparing services.

Nineteen services areas were compared and not on a single
one did Sweetwater County fare more favorably than the
former place of residence (Table B-XII). Those areas in
which the present location compared most favorably were
1) friendliness and acceptance in the community, 2) availability of television programs, and 3) the provision of
financial services (obtaining credit, etc.). Those service areas in which Sweetwater County suffered most by
comparison were 1) medical services, 2) parks, 3) suitable
housing, and 4) street maintenance (which in this case
includes traffic flows).

Green River came the closest of the three locales in
matching former locations with regard to the provision of
services. In eight service areas, Green River actually
fared better than the prior location. Those areas, in de-
creasing order of satisfaction, were as follows:

1. Availability of television programs.

2. Friendliness and acceptance in the community.

3. Fire protection.

4. A place to raise children.

5. Public transportation.

6. Sanitation services.

7. Responsiveness of local government.

8. Police protection.

Those areas in which Green River came out second best when
compared with other locations were medical services, suitable housing, and reasonable cost of living.

The comparison among rural inhabitants--on all 19 services
evaluated--always short-changed Sweetwater County. In no
single service area was the comparison even close. The
areas in which Sweetwater County received the lowest
rankings when compared with other locations were in medical services, suitable housing, street maintenance, sanitation facilities, and parks.

TABLE B-XII

Comparison of Services; Sweetwater County Versus
Preferred Location Elsewhere

	Total County		Rock Springs		Green River		Rural Areas	
	Better	Worse	Better	Worse	Better	Worse	Better	Worse
Retail stores	13%	34%	10%	24%	21%	28%	11%	57%
Medical services	7	42	7	28	12	44	6	66
Sanitation services	7	27	4	18	14	11	6	54
Availability of TV programs	13	17	10	8	22	7	10	40
Recreation facilities	10	35	7	24	21	30	6	59
Public transportation	11	23	8	14	21	16	7	47
Friendliness/acceptance in community	14	18	10	13	24	16	15	31
A place to raise children	12	30	9	21	27	22	8	55
Suitable housing	7	36	2	23	16	33	6	65
Schools/teachers	8	28	7	20	14	16	5	47
Road/street maintenance	6	35	5	23	10	30	5	62
Police protection	6	20	3	17	10	9	6	35
Fire protection	7	18	6	11	13	7	4	41
Community planning	5	29	3	23	12	20	6	48
Parks	5	37	4	27	10	28	5	58
Responsiveness of local government	5	18	4	16	15	12	3	25
Reasonable cost of living	5	32	2	21	10	31	5	52
Financial services	9	16	8	7	14	17	8	29
Outdoor recreation	12	28	9	20	18	22	14	45

Residents of Rock Springs gave two service areas better than passing marks when compared with former locations. Those two areas were in the availability of television programs and the provision of financial services. Other areas in which the comparison was minimally unfavorable were friendliness and acceptance in the community, police protection, and public transportation. Those service areas in Rock Springs which compared most unfavorably were medical services, suitable housing, community planning, road and street maintenance, and recreational facilities.

123

Nearly four out of five residents of Sweetwater County did
their grocery shopping Rock Springs and the remainder in
Green River. Even one out of five Green River residents
traveled to Rock Springs to purchase groceries. Among
rural inhabitants, 89 percent bought their groceries in
Rock Springs and 8 percent in Green River. The median
distance traveled for groceries was 1.3 miles. In Rock
Springs and Green River the average distance was a mile,
while rural residents traveled nearly seven miles to purchase groceries.

Three-fourths of the Rock Springs residents bought their
clothing in that city and 17 percent traveled as far away
as Salt Lake City to purchase clothing. Among Green River
residents, 37 percent purchased their clothing locally in
Rock Springs, 25 percent in Green River, and 26 percent in
Salt Lake City. The clothing purchasing patterns of rural
inhabitants closely resembled those of Rock Springs residents. The average inhabitant of Sweetwater County traveled nearly three miles to purchase clothing. Most Rock
Springs residents lived within a mile and a half of the
store where they normally purchase clothing, but for Green
River residents the trip averaged around 15 miles. Rural
inhabitants often traveled more than 20 miles to purchase
clothing.

Nearly 70 percent of the Sweetwater County residents found
their banking needs met in Rock Springs, while another 19
percent did their banking in Green River. All but 6 percent of the Rock Springs citizens banked locally, whereas
only 72 percent of the Green River residents did their
banking in that town. Another 14 percent traveled to Rock
Springs and 4 percent went as far as Salt Lake City. Two-
thirds of the rural residents banked in Rock Springs and
another 10 percent in Green River.

The urgent need which was expressed for improved medical
facilities (see above) is understandable when one realizes
that nearly 30 percent of the inhabitants of Sweetwater
County travel well beyond the county for routine health
care--18 percent going as far as Salt Lake for health services. One-fourth of the residents of Rock Springs had
their health care needs met in Salt Lake City, and only
two-thirds received routine medical attention locally.
Among Green River inhabitants, nearly 80 percent utilized
the medical services available in Rock Springs and Green
River, and 13 percent traveled to Salt Lake City. Two-
thirds of the rural residents went to Rock Springs for
health care and only 8 percent traveled to Salt Lake City.
However, for those rural residents the average distance
from routine health care facilities was 19 miles. For
Green River inhabitants the average distance was 12 miles,

whereas Rock Springs citizens were likely to have their health care needs met within two miles of their residence.

TABLE B-XIII

Median Distance to Most Frequently Used Services (Miles)

	Total County	Rock Springs	Green River	Rural Areas
Groceries	1.3	Less than 1	Less than 1	5.9
Clothing	2.9	1.1	15.3	12.5
Banking	1.3	Less than 1	Less than 1	7.3
Health care	3.6	1.5	12.1	19.0

Nearly half of the rural inhabitants preferred not to live that far from basic services (e.g., groceries, clothing, medical care), but were unable to find housing which was in closer proximity to those services. Also, one in seven rural residents opted for such a location because it meant being closer to work.

SUGGESTED WAYS IN WHICH LOCAL SERVICES COULD BE IMPROVED

1. *Retail services*. The principal types of stores felt to be needed in the area were 1) department stores, 2) discount or variety stores, 3) clothing stores, and 4) a grocery or supermarket. Other types of retail facilities needed were hardware stores and sporting goods outlets.

In Rock Springs, by far the major need appeared to be a department store, with secondary needs for a variety store and clothing store. There was little need for an additional supermarket in Rock Springs.

In Green River, again there was a major need for a department store, with secondary consideration given to more supermarkets and a hardware store. Other retail facilities desired in Green River included clothing stores, a discount store, and a sporting goods outlet.

Rural inhabitants indicated that by far the major needs were for a department store or a major discount operation. Individuals in the outlying areas also could use clothing stores and supermarkets.

Nearly one-third of the newcomers to the county expressed a desire for a major department store and one out of six newcomers indicated the need for a variety or discount store. Other major facilities desired by newcomers were clothing stores, grocery or supermarkets, hardware stores, sporting goods outlets, and more restaurants.

125

2. *Ways of improving medical and mental health fa-cilities*. There was a substantial desire for more doctors in the area, especially from rural inhabitants. Also, large numbers of individuals advocated a new or larger hospital--again the greatest concern being expressed in the rural areas. Individuals in the outlying locales also called for more dentists and medical specialists and felt that local medical standards and staff could be upgraded. The cry arose in Rock Springs for more doctors and a new hospital, while Green River residents advocated more clinics.

3. *Ways of improving local sanitation services*. The two major suggestions had to do with the provision of a larger, or in some areas, a new sewer plant. That need was particularly strong in Rock Springs and the rural areas. Sweetwater County residents called for more fre-quent trash collection, also a major concern among rural inhabitants. In addition, that latter group stated that water service, particularly into the trailers, should be improved. Residents of Green River were least critical of the present sanitation services.

4. *Upgrading of local broadcast facilities*. Resi-dents of Rock Springs and Green River were generally quite pleased with the present quality of television programming available. However, rural inhabitants would like to see more movies, more children's programs, more family pro-grams, and more westerns.

No particular suggestions related to improved radio pro-gramming were expressed. There was a high level of satis-faction with present programming in Rock Springs, while Green River residents would like to hear more country and western music. In the rural areas, the primary recommen-dations had to do with more rock music, more bluegrass, FM or stereo radio, and improved reception. Some resi-dents of outlying areas felt that local stations could stay on the air longer.

5. *Additional recreational facilities desired*. The most frequent suggestions concerned the need for more swimming pools and for greater development and maintenance of local parks. Also, there was substantial interest in more tennis courts (both indoor and outdoor), movie thea-ters, a bowling alley, a skating rink, golf course, and a community recreation center.

In Rock Springs, the major recreational needs centered around swimming facilities and better maintenance of the parks. In Green River, on the other hand, aside from park maintenance, the primary recreational need appeared to be a movie theater. Also, there was a great deal of inter-est in a bowling alley.

126

Improved recreational facilities would be a particular
boon to rural inhabitants. The principal recommendations
had to do with a swimming pool and the development and
maintenance of local parks and camping facilities. However, both indoor and outdoor tennis courts, as well as
more playground facilities, were also frequently mentioned.
Rural inhabitants also saw a great need for a bowling
alley and a community recreation center.

6. *Improvement of public transportation.* There was
some need expressed for a regional bus system, particularly by individuals living in the outlying areas. Also,
Green River residents would like to see a local taxis service.

7. *Ways in which greater community acceptance could
be promoted.* Residents of Rock Springs and Green River
were less likely to have suggestions for promoting a more
friendly community atmosphere than were the inhabitants of
rural areas. Many of the latter group would like to see
an alleviation of the ill feelings toward transients.
Some of them indicated that the local power structure--
especially the business community--took advantage of newcomers.

Two programs designed to ease the entry of newcomers into
the community were evaluated. The two programs--Welcome
Wagon and a referral service newcomers could telephone for
basic information about the community--were enthusiastically endorsed, especially by individuals in the rural
areas, most of whom were newcomers. The referral service
received a slightly warmer response than did the idea of a
Welcome Wagon.

8. *Improving the environment for raising children.*
The greatest problems in raising children--particularly in
the outlying areas--had to do with lack of recreational
facilities and activities to keep them out of trouble. A
number of individuals in all locations mentioned the problems of drugs and excessive drinking. Rural inhabitants
stated that the absence of trees, yards, and grass in-
hibited children's play. Residents in the outlying areas,
as well as those in Green River, complained of the lack of
parental supervision. Other complaints--voiced more frequently in the rural areas--had to do with the overcrowded
schools.

In most locations the problem was perceived as greater for
high school or junior high school age children than for
children of elementary school age. However, rural inhabitants perceived major problems among children in the latter age group also.

Despite recognition of a problem in raising children in
Sweetwater County, no single solution to the problem was

proposed. A number of individuals--particularly those living in the outlying areas--listed the need for more fa- cilities and activities for young people. Also recom- mended were more planned activities for children and better schools. Rural residents also advocated a communi- ty recreation center for young people. A number of Rock Springs residents were of the opinion that the problems could be solved by better local police control of juvenile activities.

9. *Building a better local environment for women.* Respondents were asked whether they viewed the local com- munity as being more satisfying to men or women. Both sexes agreed that the local area is more geared to men than to women. Men were more likely than women to per- ceive it as a man's community. Also, paradoxically, a greater proportion of men than women perceived it as a more satisfying environment for women. In other words, women were more apt to perceive the local community as being equally satisfying for both sexes. Individuals living in rural areas were more likely to perceive the lo- cal community as male-oriented than were residents of either of the two cities. Also, a greater proportion of individuals living in the outlying areas regarded the lo- cal community as equally unsatisfactory for both sexes.

Both men and women who perceive Sweetwater County as primarily a male environment agree it leads to the fol- lowing problems: 1) it meant that there was less for wo- men to do and 2) it leads to drinking problems. The latter problem was mentioned most often by rural residents, particularly women living in those locations. In fact, nearly 40 percent of the individuals who emphasized the local drinking problem were women living in the rural en- vironment. Few individuals in Green River mentioned the drinking problems brought on by the predominantly male en- vironment.

A number of residents of Rock Springs and the outlying areas regarded the local communities as unsafe for women at night. In those two locations there was the general opinion that the high incidence of rape and crime made the local communities dangerous for women. That opinion, how- ever, was not shared by the citizens of Green River. An- other problem was the high ratio of men to women.

As a solution to some of the sex-differentiated problems, respondents advocated more activities and clubs for women. Also frequently mentioned--particularly by women living in the outlying areas--were more activities and entertainment for married couples. Another often mentioned solution was to provide better jobs for women.

An important characteristic of any community is the general mood of its citizens. In many locations this mood is very tangible and apparent, and therefore can often be used as an accurate barometer of the direction in which the community is moving. The general community mood results from a number of interrelated factors; e.g., the degree of satisfaction with the present quality of life, the degree to which individuals sense an ability to change their community, and the level of optimism/pessimism concerning the future. The present study has attempted to measure some aspect of each of those factors, as they help to define the general mood of Sweetwater County.

In order to measure the level of satisfaction with various aspects of day-to-day life, respondents were presented with a picture of a ladder, with the top of the ladder representing the best possible situation and the bottom portraying the worst imaginable situation in a number of areas--employment, residence, family life, and overall personal satisfaction. Individuals were asked to indicate their present level of satisfaction in each instance, and also their anticipated level of satisfaction if they were still living in the area five years hence.

JOB SATISFACTION

Of the four areas measured, job satisfaction generally was rated highest (an average score countywide of 7.7, with a maximum of 10). Residents of Green River seemed to be more pleased with their present employment than did individuals living elsewhere, while rural inhabitants had the lowest job satisfaction scores.

Subgroups with higher than average job satisfaction scores were:

1. Individuals with low alienation scores (i.e., individuals with high perceived control over their personal environments).

2. Individuals with annual incomes in excess of $20,000 a year (their scores were the highest of any subgroup analyzed).

3. Individuals who expect to remain in Sweetwater County the rest of their lives.

Those groups with lower than average job satisfaction scores were:

1. Highly alienated individuals.

2. People with lower middle incomes (i.e., $7,500 to $12,500 a year).

3. Individuals who expect to leave the area within one year.

Newcomers to the area were only slightly below average in terms of job satisfaction. Although the most affluent individuals were more pleased with their jobs than any other economic subgroup, there was not a linear relationship between income levels and job satisfaction. The low income and upper middle income groups had average scores, whereas the lower middle income category exhibited as much job dissatisfaction as any of the subgroups analyzed.

There was something of a perceived "dead-end" quality about the job situation in Sweetwater County. On the average, individuals did not expect to find greater job satisfaction in five years than at present. Expectations varied, of course. For example, there was an anticipated increase in job satisfaction in Rock Springs, and job levels were viewed as nearly static over a five year period by inhabitants of the rural areas. However, in Green River future expectations with regard to the job were actually lower than present levels. Newcomers, particularly those living in Green River, had lower job expectations for the future. Also, highly alienated individuals had lower expectations with regard to job satisfaction in the future.

LEVEL OF SATISFACTION WITH PRESENT LIVING QUARTERS

Satisfaction scores in this area were the lowest of the four life areas studied. The level of discontent with the individual's present dwelling was extremely high among rural inhabitants.

Those subgroups with higher than average levels of satisfaction with their present homes were:

1. Individuals who expect to live in Sweetwater County the rest of their lives.

2. Residents of permanent, single family homes.

3. Individuals with low alienation scores.

4. Citizens of Rock Springs and Green River.

5. Women.

Those subgroups which exhibited a high level of discontent with their present housing were:

1. Newcomers.

2. Inhabitants of outlying areas.

3. Mobile home dwellers.

4. Individuals who anticipate leaving the area within one year.

5. People who list the need for housing as a high priority.

6. Highly alienated individuals.

7. Men.

There were no high expectations that the housing situation would improve dramatically within five years. Average scores in anticipated satisfaction with housing rose only slightly. The greatest increase occurred in Rock Springs. However, in both Green River and the outlying areas, there was no anticipated increase in level of satisfaction with housing facilities.

There were slight anticipated increases among individuals who ranked housing as a high priority item, among both trailer dwellers and residents of permanent, single family homes, and among both men and women. People with low alienation scores (i.e., those individuals who perceived themselves as having a great deal of control over their immediate environment) expressed the greatest optimism regarding the adequacy of future housing. Newcomers, on the other hand, particularly those living in Green River, foresaw no favorable changes in housing conditions over the five year period.

SATISFACTION WITH FAMILY LIFE

With the exception of Green River residents, individuals generally agreed that their family's satisfaction level would increase within five years. The anticipated increase was highest in the rural areas, which have (and anticipate continuing to have) the lowest level of satisfaction.

Table B-XIV illustrates comparative indices of satisfaction.

DESIRE TO REMAIN IN THE AREA

Another measure of satisfaction with the present way of life in Sweetwater County was the anticipated length of residence in the county. It makes sense to assume that individuals who were very unhappy with the area would not expect to remain for a substantial period of time. A majority of the Sweetwater County residents indicated that

131

TABLE B-XIV

Indices of Satisfaction

	Average Scores[a]			
	Total County	Rock Springs	Green River	Rural Areas
Present job satisfaction	7.7	7.7	8.1	7.1
Anticipated job satisfaction in 5 years	7.7	8.1	7.8	7.2
Satisfaction with present home	6.6	7.0	6.9	5.4
Anticipated satisfaction with home in 5 years	6.8	7.5	6.9	5.4
Present satisfaction with family life	6.9	7.1	7.6	6.2
Anticipated satisfaction with family life in 5 years	7.2	7.3	7.5	6.5

[a]No scores available for comparison.

they would probably spend more than five years in the area, with 45 percent expecting to spend the rest of their lives there. Approximately one out of six individuals would be leaving within one year. In the rural areas, where the median anticipated length of residence was only slightly more than two years, 36 percent of the inhabitants expected to remain less than one year.

The people with the shortest residency expectations (all approximately two years in length) were newcomers, career construction workers, and individuals who had moved frequently within the last five years. Also, mobile home dwellers had an average residence expectancy of only 3.3 years. Only 24 percent of the newcomers and a like percentage of the highly mobile individuals would expect to stay in the county for more than five years. Nearly three-fourths of the career construction employees would expect to be moving somewhere else within that five year period.

The major reasons for leaving within a year were job-related (28 percent), a desire to return to a prior place of residence (11 percent), and a general dislike of the area (11 percent). Those individuals who expected to remain from one to five years generally indicated that they would stay as long as the job lasted, but that their job expectations did not exceed five years. Also, 17 percent reported that they would go where the employment opportunities existed or they were transferred. A similar

132

percentage of the individuals with intermediate residence expectations reported that they preferred other locations to Sweetwater County.

The future availability of suitable housing would certainly play a major role in determining whether or not people left the area. Whereas 22 percent of the individuals in the county indicated that their chances of remaining in Wyoming--if suitable housing were available--were 50-50 or less, if such housing were not provided, 37 percent would fall into the low probability category. In other words, housing appeared to be a determining factor in the decision to stay for about 15 percent of the county population.

Housing was even more critical to the inhabitants of rural areas. Even with suitable housing, 42 percent of those inhabitants would fall in the minimal probability category. Without such housing, however, 64 percent indicated that there was a 50-50 chance or less that they would remain in the area--a difference of 22 percent under the two sets of conditions.

To give additional meaning to the previously noted housing priority (see previous section), it is interesting to examine the residence expectancies of individuals who ranked housing among the top five priority items. Among that group--particularly residents of Rock Springs--the availability of suitable housing would be critical in their decision to remain in the area.

With suitable housing, about half of the career construction workers would be a good bet to leave the area. However, without such housing, over three-fourths of them would have a low probability of remaining--a difference of better than 25 percent attributable to the availability of suitable housing.

PRESENT DWELLING PATTERNS

DESCRIPTION OF PRESENT HOME

More than 60 percent of the residents of Sweetwater County lived in permanent, single family dwellings; nearly one-third lived in trailers; and another 4 percent resided in apartments. The distribution of the types of dwelling units differed markedly from location to location. For example, in Rock Springs, seven out of eight individuals lived in single family homes, 7 percent in trailers, and 6 percent in apartments. In Green River, single family homes still predominated (71 percent); however, 20 percent of the residents lived in trailers. Trailers abounded in the rural areas, where they constituted 81 percent of the dwelling units. In the more isolated areas, only 15 percent of the population lived in permanent, single family homes.

Countywide, more than 60 percent of the recent arrivals lived in mobile homes. However, a majority of the newcomers to both Rock Springs and Green River lived in permanent, single family dwellings. Nearly 30 percent occupied trailers and roughly 16 percent lived in apartments. However, in the outlying areas, seven out of eight newcomers lived in trailers, with only 9 percent in permanent housing. In every location, as length of residence in the area increased, there was a greater likelihood that the individual would live somewhere other than a mobile home.

The housing patterns of newcomers in the major employment groups were also examined. At least one-third of the trona miners and newcomers in other employment categories --with the exception of career construction workers--occupied permanent, single family housing. Only 18 percent of the newly arrived career construction workers lived in permanent housing, whereas 77 percent occupied mobile homes.

TABLE B-XV

Type of Dwelling Unit

	Total County	Rock Springs	Green River	Rural Areas
Permanent, single family home	63%	87%	71%	15%
Mobile home	31	7	20	81
Apartment	4	6	6	0
Other type of dwelling	2	0	3	4

Since there is often an inferential (if not real) distinction made between those individuals who live in permanent, single family housing and those who live in mobile homes, it is worthwhile to compare the characteristics of the two types of dwellers.

1. *Residents of permanent housing.* The average occupancy of a single family dwelling was 3.4 persons. Slightly more than 80 percent were married, 11 percent either widowed or divorced, and 7 percent were single. The majority of the permanent home dwellers were long time residents of the area. The educational level of these individuals was somewhat higher than that of the mobile home dwellers. Seventeen percent of the residents of permanent housing had graduated from college, with 8 percent in the post graduate category. One-fourth of the individuals had

134

not received a high school diploma. Their median income
was slightly in excess of $13,000 a year, with 14 percent
earning less than $5,000 a year and 17 percent having sal-
aries in excess of $20,000 a year.

2. *Mobile home dwellers*. The average number of residents per housing unit was actually slightly larger than
that of the permanent home dwellers. However, the difference was not significant. Eighty-nine percent of the mobile home residents were married; 3 percent were either
divorced or widowed; and 8 percent were single. Only 7
percent of the individuals living in mobile homes could be
considered long time residents of Sweetwater County.

Ten percent of the individuals had graduated from college
and 31 percent had not finished high school. Despite
their relatively low educational level, their median income ($14,000) was actually higher than that of the resi-
dents of permanent homes. Only 4 percent of the mobile
home dwellers had annual incomes less than $5,000, and 18
percent earned in excess of $20,000 a year.

TABLE B-XVI

Demographic Characteristics of Residents of Various
Types of Dwelling Units

	All Dwelling Units	Permanent, Single Family Homes	Mobile Homes
Marital Status			
Married	82%	81%	89%
Single	9	7	8
Divorced or widowed	10	11	3
Average number of residents per unit	3.4	3.4	3.5
Educational Level			
Did not graduate from high school	28%	25%	31%
High school graduates	73	75	68
College graduates	15	17	10
Income Level			
Less than $7,500	17%	20%	9%
$20,000 and over	16	17	18
Median income	$13,209	$13,056	$14,018

Homeowners outnumbered renters by better than three to one
in the county, with the highest percentage of home ownership occurring in Rock Springs (82 percent). Mobile homes
were usually owned, rather than rented. However, in Green
River there was a high percentage (41 percent) of mobile
homes being rented. Nearly two-thirds of the newly arrived career construction employees owned their mobile
homes.

In the entire county, the average (median) length of home
occupancy was 3.3 years. Nearly one-third of the individuals had lived in their present homes less than one year
and approximately half had lived there less than three
years. The average length of occupancy was highest in
Rock Springs (6.4 years) and well under a year in outlying
areas. In Green River, the average length of occupancy
was 4.1 years.

The turnover in mobile home occupancy was extremely high,
particularly in the rural areas. Countywide, well over 50
percent of the mobile home dwellers had lived in their
present units less than one year. In the rural areas, 86
percent of the mobile home dwellers had occupied their
present units less than three years (63 percent less than
one year). The average length of occupancy in permanent
housing in both Rock Springs and Green River was roughly
seven to eight years.

In the town of Rock Springs, 85 percent of the trona
miners lived in permanent, single family housing, and 8
percent each in apartments and mobile homes. The proportion of mobile home and apartment dwellers among career
construction workers in Rock Springs was much higher.
Eighteen percent of the latter group of workers lived in
mobile homes, 14 percent in apartments, and slightly more
than two-thirds in permanent housing. In Green River, 36
percent of the trona miners lived either in mobile homes
(26 percent) or apartments (10 percent). In the outlying
areas, 90 percent of the career construction workers lived
in mobile homes.

The typical dwelling in the county had two and a half bedrooms and one bathroom. Homes in Rock Springs had the
highest average number of bedrooms (2.7), while homes in
outlying areas had the fewest bedrooms (an average of two
per dwelling unit). Roughly 60 percent of the permanent,
single family dwellings had three or more bedrooms. Mobile homes generally averaged two bedrooms, except in
Green River where well over half of the mobile home units
had three or more bedrooms. Those larger mobile homes
also were more likely to have two bathrooms.

The average home in Sweetwater County cost $14,560 at the
time of purchase, which was generally about two years ago.
Purchase price varied markedly from location to location.
In Rock Springs, the average home cost $19,130 at time of
purchase; in Green River, the average purchase price was
$16,430; and in the outlying areas the average purchase
price was $9,545. The low latter figure in rural areas
reflected the high proportion of mobile homes which averaged $9,400 at the time of purchase.

Homeowners in Sweetwater County made an average of $150 a
month in house payments. Mobile homeowners made average
monthly payments of approximately $135, and permanent,
single family homeowners averaged approximately $190 a
month in house payments. The average rental unit in the
county cost slightly more than $150 a month.

INITIAL DIFFICULTIES IN FINDING HOUSING

Despite admitted housing shortages, over half of the residents of Sweetwater County reported having had no difficulty finding housing. However, 20 percent indicated that
they had arrived prior to the present boom, thereby es-
caping the headache. On the negative side, 20 percent reported having encountered a great deal of difficulty, and
14 percent indicated that it took more time than desired
to find suitable housing. Many newcomers indicated that
the situation was alleviated by knowing someone who assisted them in locating housing.

The acute nature of the problem was underscored by the
fact that newcomers experienced a great deal of difficulty
locating suitable housing; in fact, twice as many newcomers as long time residents reported having had initial
problems with housing. Nearly 20 percent of the rural
residents had difficulty finding trailer space. The most
troublesome location appeared to be Green River, where 41
percent of the newcomers said that their present home was
not their first choice, and that they would have preferred
something else.

EVALUATION OF PRESENT HOUSING

Individuals were asked to list the benefits of living in
their present homes. Ownership alone was one of the major
perceived advantages of present home occupancy, particularly among citizens of Rock Springs and Green River. Individuals in those two towns also praised the neighborhoods in which they lived--a factor, however, rarely cited

by rural inhabitants. Rock Springs residents also mentioned the roominess of the house as being a definite plus factor. Mobile home owners--especially those living in outlying areas--preferred the mobility which such housing provided. That benefit was mentioned by 30 percent of the mobile homeowners.

TABLE B-XVII

Advantages of Present Home

	Total County	Rock Springs	Green River	Rural Areas
Owns home	24%	28%	26%	17%
Likes the neighborhood	22	30	26	4
Large; roomy	11	14	7	8
Mobility; can move it easily	9	2	4	25
Quality of home; well built	8	11	9	1
Quiet; privacy	8	8	11	7
No perceived advantages	7	7	7	8
Inexpensive	6	5	6	10
Close to work	5	2	2	12
Close to schools	5	7	7	0

The principal housing complaints centered around the lack of space (15 percent) and the need for maintenance and repair (12 percent). Nearly one-third of the residents of the area expressed satisfaction with their present housing. Newcomers had more housing complaints than did long time residents. Recent arrivals in the area--particularly those living in Green River and the outlying areas--voiced dissatisfaction with the shortage of space and overcrowded conditions. Also high on the list of overall complaints was the constant dirt and dust in the area. Newcomers to Rock Springs had specific criticisms of their present neighborhoods. Only 2 percent of the residents of the county and less than 10 percent of the newcomers grumbled about the high cost of housing. Seven percent of the newcomers living in rural areas complained about inadequate plumbing or the lack of running water.

Much of the dissatisfaction with present housing conditions emanated from mobile homeowners, whose major complaints centered around their crowded conditions. The omnipresent dirt and dust were a source of dissatisfaction to both mobile homeowners and permanent home residents living in the outlying areas. One in five of the individuals who had expectations for remaining in the area for a short period of time criticized their present dwelling as

being rundown and in need of repair. However, cramped
living conditions still rated high on the complaint list,
particularly in rural areas.

DESIRED HOUSING CONDITIONS

Housing preferences were analyzed in several ways. First,
individuals were asked to describe the kind of home and
neighborhood they would like to live in at the present
time--given the Sweetwater environment and the practicali-
ties imposed by the present money market. After those
choices were thoroughly explored, each individual was presented with six pictures (see pages 177-179) of actual
housing available in the area. Two pictures portrayed
single family, permanent dwellings (one older and one
quite new); two were photographs of mobile homes; and two
were pictures of new apartment units. Individuals were
asked to choose the most preferable alternative, as well
as the least attractive type of housing, and discuss the
rationale behind those choices.

DESCRIPTION OF IDEAL HOME

Nearly half of the residents of the area mentioned--on a
spontaneous basis--that they preferred to own their own
homes. Only 6 percent of the respondents indicated that a
rental would be ideal, with many of those individuals
living in mobile homes in the rural areas. The desirability of home ownership was highest in Green River and among
mobile home dwellers in every location. Permanent home
dwellers in Rock Springs were least likely to mention ownership, perhaps because they took it for granted. All of
the career construction employees in Green River, and over
40 percent of them in Rock Springs and the outlying areas,
regarded home ownership as particularly desirable.

Permanent housing was chosen over mobile homes by a margin
of nearly seven to one, with the major interest in mobile
homes coming from the rural residents. Only a handful of
individuals regarded a high density dwelling unit such as
an apartment, townhouse, or condominium as acceptable.

The principal amenities mentioned in spontaneous fashion
had to do with some type of landscaping. For example,
nearly one-third of the respondents mentioned the need for
grass; 30 percent desired a yard; and 27 percent mentioned
trees. The need for greenery was less pronounced in Rock
Springs than anywhere else and was paramount among rural
dwellers. Nearly 10 percent of the county (particularly
residents of Green River and outlying areas) desired a

garden. Paved streets were mentioned frequently, both in
Green River and rural locations. A significant number of
individuals (approximately 25 percent) in those two locations also wanted garages. Available water was seen as a
significant amenity. Close access to work, schools, and
other facilities did not appear to be as important as some
of the earlier mentioned factors. Certainly, close proximity to work was not a key factor in home selection.

Approximately a 20 percent increase in present bedroom capacity would be desirable in a new home. The average
(mean) number of bedrooms needed was 3.0, with very little
variation between subgroups or locations. That figure
represented about one additional bedroom per dwelling unit
for trailer dwellers who, as noted earlier, often complained about cramped living conditions. Only 15 percent
of all residents expressed a need for more than three bedrooms. An additional bathroom--that is, two instead of
one--also was felt to be extremely desirable, particularly
by mobile home dwellers.

A reasonable commuting distance to work was seen as about
14 miles, or perhaps 15 to 20 minutes driving time. That
figure varied a good deal from location to location, with
Rock Springs residents regarding nine miles as reasonable,
Green River residents seeing 16 miles as within reason,
and rural inhabitants willing to travel as much as 19
miles one way to work. Trailer dwellers in every location
did not consider a commute in excess of 20 miles as being
unreasonable. A commute of such length was generally regarded as quite acceptable by both career construction
workers and trona miners. White-collar workers were least
likely to be willing to travel greater distances to work.

COST CONSIDERATIONS

As noted above, respondents were requested to describe
their ideal housing situation in Sweetwater County within
a realistic framework. A major element of that framework
was the ability of individuals to pay for the type of
housing which he or she described. After specifying their
ideal housing situation, respondents were asked to indicate the amount they would be willing to pay to obtain
such housing. The mean figure countywide was slightly in
excess of $200 a month, ranging from a high of $225 a
month in Rock Springs to about $200 a month in outlying
areas. That meant that Sweetwater County residents would
be willing to pay approximately one-third more than their
present monthly payment in order to obtain suitable
housing (i.e., $204 a month versus the present $150 a
month in housing payments). For mobile home dwellers, that
increase would even be more dramatic--in the neighborhood
of 45 percent more per month for housing.

140

The average rental payment for desirable housing was approximately $190 a month, versus the present average of $150 per month in rental payments. In other words, individuals would be willing to spend slightly less for ideal rental housing than if it were owned. However, even on a rental basis, residents would tolerate approximately a 25 percent increase in housing costs, provided suitable housing were available.

TABLE B-XVIII

Housing Characteristics Desired

	Total County	Rock Springs	Green River	Rural Areas
Number of bedrooms desired	3.0	2.9	3.0	2.9
Median monthly payments regarded as acceptable (homeowners)	$204	$223	$213	$198
Median rent regarded as acceptable	$187	$173	$185	$188

CHOICES AMONG HOUSING ALTERNATIVES

Of the six housing alternatives analyzed, only two--the two permanent, single family homes--held any widespread appeal. The older, well-landscaped (e.g., trees and lawn) home (choice B) was preferred by 28 percent of the residents. The newer home which also had a lawn and shrubbery, but no trees (choice D), was selected by 26 percent of the individuals. However, 40 percent of all individuals in the sample were not asked to rate the alternatives because of their expressed satisfaction with their present housing. By far the greatest proportion of those non-respondents were residing in Rock Springs. Newcomers--especially those in Green River and the outlying areas where housing shortages are more critical--showed a very high preference for the two permanent homes.

There was really very little to choose between the two permanent housing alternatives--choices B and D--except that newcomers leaned slightly toward the newer, modern home. However, among the individuals for whom suitable housing was a critical factor in their decision to remain in the area, either type of permanent housing was regarded as suitable. Also, all employment groups (e.g., trona miners, career construction workers) in all locations had strong preferences for the two permanent housing alternatives. Lower income individuals generally preferred the

141

older home, whereas other income groups showed no preference between the two permanent housing choices.

The reasons underlying any housing choice were generally
either the landscaping or a preference for the style of
home. Those two features were particularly appealing to
rural residents who once again expressed their needs for
trees, grass, and suitable landscaping. They also were
attuned to features which provided more space and to the
existence of a garage. Choice B--the older home--was generally preferred because of its excellent landscaping and
its style. Also, residents of Rock Springs and the rural
areas were attracted by its privacy and lack of close proximity to neighboring homes. Choice D--the newer home--ap-
pealed to people for a number of reasons, primarily the
following: 1) its style and overall appearance; 2) the
excellent landscaping; 3) its garage; and 4) its apparent
large size. In addition, the newer home was cited as ap-
pearing substantial and of high quality.

Opinion as to the least suitable housing was much more
varied. However, one finding appeared to be fairly clear-
cut--residents looked upon high density apartment structures with much more disfavor than they did on mobile
homes. The two apartment units pictured--choices A and F
--received the highest number of negative mentions (18
percent and 17 percent, respectively). Next in terms of
disfavor were the two photos of mobile home units--choices
C and E. Individuals who reported the chances were excellent of their staying in the area provided suitable
housing were available also had strong negative feelings
towards mobile home dwellings.

Present trailer residents did not have as strong negative
reactions towards mobile homes as did permanent home dwellers. Trailer residents exhibited a marked dislike for
choice A--a very stark high density dwelling unit. That
alternative also was ill-regarded by people who expected
to leave Sweetwater County within several years. Women
had particularly negative feelings about choice A.

Present mobile home dwellers found the mobile home alternative (choice C) which was located in a more verdant
setting to be more desirable than the mobile home which
was virtually devoid of landscaping (choice E).

The most distasteful aspects of those negative housing
choices were as follows: 1) lack of privacy/congestion;
2) a general dislike of mobile homes; and 3) a general
dislike of apartments. Complaints about the lack of privacy were particularly prevalent in Green River and the
outlying areas.

The specific criticisms of the individual units pictured
were as follows:

1. Alternative A (high density apartment unit)
    - Lacks privacy; congestion
    - Dislike apartment living
    - Lack of landscaping
    - No yard or playground
2. Alternative C (mobile home)
    - Dislike of mobile homes and trailer parks
    - Small size; no storage space
    - No yard or playground
3. Alternative E (mobile home)
    - Dislike of mobile home
    - Lack of privacy
    - No landscaping
4. Alternative F (high density apartment unit)
    - Lack of privacy
    - Dislike of apartment living
    - Lack of storage space and small size

TABLE B-XIX

Ratings of Housing Alternatives

	Total County	Rock Springs	Green River	Rural Areas
Picture A				
Desirable	9%	6%	13%	9%
Undesirable	33	21	39	48
Picture B				
Desirable	54	32	84	70
Undesirable	1	1	1	3
Picture C				
Desirable	9	5	14	13
Undesirable	24	17	40	22
Picture D				
Desirable	51	30	75	66
Undesirable	3	2	2	5
Picture E				
Desirable	6	3	9	9
Undesirable	33	24	56	31
Picture F				
Desirable	8	5	9	10
Undesirable	36	26	49	41

Looking at only the housing needs of present mobile home dwellers, the future availability of permanent, single family housing appears to be a critical factor in the

stability of the community. The availability of such
housing represents the "swing" factor for about 30 percent
of the mobile home residents. In other words, if such
housing is not provided, an additional 30 percent of those
residents--over and above the number who would leave for
other reasons--would depart Sweetwater County. Besides
that 30 percent, another 20 percent would prefer permanent,
single family housing to mobile home living, although for
them the difference is not as critical. Therefore, approximately one-half of the present mobile home dwellers
would be in the market for permanent housing.

RESIDENTS' LIFE STYLES

ACTIVITIES ENGAGED IN

Each respondent was given a list of 38 activities and
asked to respond to them in two ways: 1) the frequency
with which they engaged in each of those activities and
2) their preference, on a five point scale, for each of
the listed activities. The second measure provided a means
of determining the interest in activities which are
presently unavailable in Sweetwater County.

By far the two most frequently engaged-in activities--by
roughly two-thirds of the residents of the county--were 1)
reading books and magazines for pleasure and 2) visiting
neighbors and friends. Reading was a much more frequent
activity in rural areas than it was in either Rock Springs
or in Green River. Also, visiting neighbors and friends
occurred more frequently in the rural areas than in the
two cities. In the former location, 57 percent indicated
that they visited friends two or three times a week or
more, compared with 35 percent of the city dwellers who
engaged in similar activities that frequently.

Following those two major activities, there was a large
drop-off in frequency for other major pastimes. A list of
the top ten activities (with the percentage engaging in
each at least once a week) is shown in Table B-XX.

Fishing and hunting were the two major sports in the area.
Following those two outdoor sports in terms of frequency
of participation were camping, hiking, pistol and rifle
shooting, boating, and bowling. Very few individuals
played handball, tennis, or golf.

Among other activities infrequently engaged in were
working in local politics, playing team sports, attending
symphonies and plays, and volunteer work.

144

TABLE B-XX

Top Ten Activities

Activity	Percent
1. Reading a book/magazine	70%
2. Visiting friend or neighbor	67
3. Going to church	35
4. Gardening	34
5. Special hobbies	26
6. Fishing	24
7. Going out to dinner	23
8. Hunting	22
9. Playing games and cards with friends	21
10. Entertaining at home	20

The ten most frequently engaged-in activities also constituted the ten most preferred activities for Sweetwater
County residents, although not necessarily in the order
reported above. The two most preferred activities--
reading books and magazines and visiting neighbors and
friends--were also the two activities most frequently
pursued. However, going out to dinner--an activity which
was listed seventh in frequency--rated very high on the
preference scale. In other words, it appears that local
residents would enjoy dining out more than they presently
do.

TABLE B-XXI

Ten Most Enjoyable Activities

Activity	Average Preference Rating[a]
1. Reading books and magazines	1.6
2. Visiting neighbors and friends	1.7
3. Going out to dinner	1.9
4. Camping	2.0
5. Fishing	2.1
6. Gardening	2.2
7. Entertaining at home	2.2
8. Going to church	2.3
9. Playing games and cards with friends	2.3
10. Special hobbies	2.4

[a]Ratings varied from 1=most preferable to 5=least preferable. Therefore, low scores indicate enjoyable activities and scores greater than three indicate activities
which have a somewhat negative valence.

145

Of all 38 activities, "working in local politics" was given the least favorable rating (3.6). In none of the three locations did political work hold any appeal. The other activities which rated on the negative side of the scale were as follows:

2. Handball (3.4)
3. Golf (3.3)
4. Going to a bar (3.2)
5. Playing pool or billiards (3.1)
6. Attending a civic meeting (3.1)
7. Attending a fraternal or club function (3.1)
8. Tennis (3.1)
9. Playing a team sport (3.1)
10. Roping, riding, and rodeo (3.1)

INTEREST IN ADULT AND VOCATIONAL EDUCATION COURSES

Over 90 percent of the residents of the county were aware that there were local facilities for adult and vocational education. Roughly 80 percent of the individuals identi-fied Western Wyoming Junior College in Rock Springs as the location of those educational facilities.

Approximately 35 percent of the individuals were either "extremely interested" or "quite interested" in taking college level or adult education courses. Balancing that were the 43 percent who were not at all interested in such courses. Interest in such courses seemed to be lower in Green River than in either Rock Springs or the rural areas. Newcomers were much more interested in such courses than were long time residents of Sweetwater County. Individu-als with expectations of remaining in the area from one to five years had the greatest interest in adult education --over 50 percent of them being either "extremely" or "quite" interested. The interest levels of men and women were about equal.

Those people with very high scores on the alienation scale were twice as likely to have a strong interest in adult education as were individuals with very low scores on the scale. Perhaps that indicates a desire on the part of people who regard themselves as outside the power struc-ture to improve their overall skills and thus become more adept at manipulating their personal environment.

Long work hours and the shortage of free time were given as the principal inhibitors of attendance at adult educa-tion courses. Those reasons prevailed in all three loca-tions. Citizens of Green River indicated that poor driv-ing conditions often prevented them from attending as frequently as they wished. They also blamed the lack of babysitting facilities as a major deterrent to attendance.

146

That reason was also given by a substantial number of rural inhabitants, who also complained of the lack of transportation. In only a handful of instances were cost factors or curriculum inadequacies given as reasons for poor attendance.

COMMITMENT TO COMMUNITY

In an effort to determine the degree of gregariousness and interest in community affairs, several descriptions of types of families and individuals were read to respondents. They were then asked to indicate how well each of the descriptions fit them.

Slightly more than 40 percent of the Sweetwater County residents described themselves as liking to socialize a lot with the neighbors. Only 24 percent did not regard such a description as applicable. Green River residents, more than inhabitants of the other two locations, described themselves as being gregarious in this regard.

More than half of the residents of the county were not interested in becoming deeply involved in community affairs. That disinterest in the community was particularly evident among 1) rural inhabitants, 2) long time residents of Rock Springs, 3) individuals who expected to leave the area within a short period of time, and somewhat surprisingly, 4) women.

Rural inhabitants exhibited much more wanderlust than did city residents, particularly those living in Rock Springs. For example, well over half of the inhabitants of the outlying areas indicated that they disliked being tied down too long in one spot. In contrast, less than 25 percent of the citizens of Rock Springs described themselves in such a manner. Generally, men showed less rootedness than did women.

Approximately two-thirds of the residents of the county indicated that they liked to go out a lot and have a good time. Residents of Green River and the outlying areas appeared to be more interested in going out than did Rock Springs citizens. Also, women reported a greater preference for staying at home than did the men in the sample.

147

Degree of Fit with Statements Describing Various
Social Activities

	Total County	Rock Springs	Green River	Rural Areas
Likes to socialize a lot with the neighbors.				
Fits very well	41%	40%	47%	41%
Describes somewhat	33	30	40	34
Does not fit	24	29	14	25
The type of person who gets deeply involved in community affairs.				
Fits very well	13	14	15	10
Describes somewhat	34	33	37	33
Does not fit	52	52	48	57
Don't like to be tied down too long in one spot.				
Fits very well	20	14	24	29
Describes somewhat	20	13	21	27
Does not fit	60	71	55	42
Likes to go out a lot and have a good time.				
Fits very well	36	31	40	43
Describes somewhat	31	32	33	29
Does not fit	30	33	23	25
Prefers not to mix too much with the neighbors.				
Fits very well	13	10	17	14
Describes somewhat	31	26	34	38
Does not fit	55	62	48	46
Enjoys having lots of children playing close by in the neighborhood.				
Fits very well	33	34	31	32
Describes somewhat	35	32	37	38
Does not fit	31	32	32	29

NEEDS ASSESSMENT SURVEY QUESTIONNAIRE

Questionnaire Number_____

Interviewer Number_____

Time of Interview: _____AM or PM

WYOMING QUESTIONNAIRE

	. DECK ONE

1. How many years have you lived in Sweetwater County?

1 Under 1 year	6 5-9.9 years
2 1-1.9 years	7 10-19.9 years
3 2-2.9 years	8 20 years or more
4 3-3.9 years	9 Don't know
5 4-4.9 years	

A1 ___

(IF RESPONDENT ANSWERS "ALL HIS/HER LIFE", ASK AGE AND RECORD IN SPACE ABOVE)

IF ANSWER TO Q. 1 IS "1-5": 1a. How many times in the past five years have you moved from one city to another?

_____

A2 ___

2. How many years have you lived in Wyoming?

1 Under 1 year	6 5-9.9 years
2 1-1.9 years	7 10-19.9 years
3 2-2.9 years	8 20 years or more
4 3-3.9 years	9 Don't know
5 4-4.9 years	

A3 ___

3. Are you married?

1 Married
2 Divorced/Separated
3 Widowed
4 Never married (single)

A4 ___

IF MARRIED: 3a. Do you have your family here with you now?

1 Yes   2 No

A5 ___

IF NO TO Q. 3a: 3b. Why isn't your family here?

(2 MENTIONS)

A6 ___
A7 ___

4. How many people live in this household? _____

A8 ___

5. What are their ages? (RECORD AGES OF ALL HOUSEHOLD MEMBERS)

___ ___ ___ ___ ___ ___ ___ ___ ___ ___ ___ ___

A9 ___
A10 ___
A11 ___

151

6. Do you have any children in school here?   1__Yes 2__No   . A12 ___

   IF YES TO Q. 6: 6a. What activities do your children participate in?   (3 MENTIONS)
                (4-H, Paper Route, Sports)

       _____ _____   A13 ___

       _____ _____ __   A14 ___

       _____ _____   A15 ___

7. What, in your opinion, are the three most pressing problems facing the local area here?

   1. _____   A16,17 ___ ___

     _____

   2. _____   A18,19 ___ ___

     _____

   3. _____   A20,21 ___ ___

     _____

   7a. How would you recommend solving the problem of (1ST NAMED PROBLEM   (2 MENTIONS
      ABOVE)? (REPEAT FOR EACH PROBLEM NAMED)   EACH)

      _____   A22,23 ___ ___

      _____   A24,25 ___ ___

      _____

   7b. Solution to second-named problem?_____   A26,27 ___ ___

      _____   A28,29 ___ ___

      _____

   7c. Solution to third-named problem?_____   A30,31 ___ ___

      _____   A32,33 ___ ___

      _____

8. In general, do you feel that life in (NAME OF COMMUNITY) is improving, that it's staying about the same, or that it's going downhill?

      1___Improving   3___The same-positive   5___Downhill
      2___The same   4___The same-negative   6___Don't know

    IF DOWNHILL: 8a. Why do you feel that life is going downhill?

A34 ___

(2 MENTIONS)

A35,36 ___ ___

A37,38 ___ ___

9. In your day-to-day life what do you consider to be the most rewarding or enjoyable aspects of living in this area? (PROBE)

(3 MENTIONS)

A39,40 ___ ___

A41,42 ___ ___

A43,44 ___ ___

153

10. Now I'd like to ask you several questions about how you feel about various problem areas and issues? Do you often tend to feel that: (READ STATEMENTS)

	1 Yes	2 No	3 Don't Know	
a. Tax laws are written to help the rich and not the average man.	___	___	___	A45 ___
b. The rich get richer and the poor get poorer.	___	___	___	A46 ___
c. What I think doesn't really count much.	___	___	___	A47 ___
d. People who are running this state don't care what happens to people like me.	___	___	___	A48 ___
e. People with power are out to take advantage of me.	___	___	___	A49 ___
f. I feel left out of things around here.	___	___	___	A50 ___

Total Score (See Code)　　　　　　　　A51 ___

11. Here is a picture of a ladder which represents your level of satisfaction with various aspects of your day-to-day life. (HAND RESPONDENT CARD A) Suppose we say that the top of the ladder (POINT TO VALUE 10) represents the best possible situation and the bottom represents the worst imaginable situation for you. Where would you put yourself on the ladder with regard to your (YOUR HUSBAND'S) present job? From the best possible job situation to the worst--where does your (HIS) present job fit in?

　　　　　　　　　　　　　　　_____　　A52,53 ___ ___

11a. And if you are still living here five years from now--where would you imagine your (HIS) job satisfaction would rate?

　　　　　　　　　　　　　　　_____　　A54,55 ___ ___

11b. Where would you put yourself on the ladder with regard to your present home? From the most desirable residence to the least-- where does your present home fit in?

　　　　　　　　　　　　　　　_____　　A56,57 ___ ___

11c. And if you continue to live in this area, in five years where would you imagine you would rate your satisfaction with your home at that time--from most desirable to least?

　　　　　　　　　　　　　　　_____　　A58,59 ___ ___

154

11d. In terms of your entire family's satisfaction with life around here, where would you rate their satisfaction on the ladder?

_____   A60,61 ___ ___

11e. And where would you expect your family's satisfaction level to be five years from now, provided you're still living here?

_____   A62,63 ___ ___

12. In terms of your personal overall satisfaction with your present life, where would you rate it on the ladder?

_____   A64,65 ___ ___

12a. And where on that ladder--if you continue to live in this area-- would you expect your personal overall satisfaction with your way of life to be?

_____   A66,67 ___ ___

IF ANSWER TO Q. 12a IS LOWER THAN ANSWER TO Q.12 :

13. Why would you expect to be less satisfied with your life around here in five years?

(2 MENTIONS)

A68,69 ___ ___

A70,71 ___ ___

A72 ___
A73 ___
A74 ___
A75 ___
A76 ___

A77 _1_

(THREE DIGIT RESPONDENT NUMBER) A78-80 ___ ___ ___

END DECK 1

155

14. (HAND RESPONDENT GOLD SHEET) Listed on that sheet are 13 services or facilities which are available in most communities. When some of those items are missing or deficient, they become problem areas. I'd like you to rank the five items on that list from 1 to 5 in terms of the need to make (NAME OF COMMUNITY) the kind of place where you'd want to stay. For example, the top priority area in need of a solution would be ranked "1", the second priority area would be ranked "2", and so on to 5. Please make your rankings in Column A on the sheet.

(WAIT FOR RESPONDENT TO COMPLETE RANKING)

Now look at the remaining eight items on the list. Please choose the three items which you would give least priority to and mark those with the number 13 in Column A.

14a. Now go back through the list and place an "X" in Column B beside those items which definitely would need improvement before you would consider remaining here permanently.

___Would not consider remaining under any circumstances
B40 ___

14b. When we talk about solving local problems, it usually means additional expense to the local residents in terms of taxes, fees, and so forth. I'd like you to rank from 1 to 5 the problem areas on that sheet in terms of the public costs of solving them. In other words, the most costly problem to solve would be ranked "1", second most costly "2", and so forth to 5. Please record your rankings in Column C on the sheet. (INTERVIEWER: BE CERTAIN THAT ONLY FIVE OF THE 13 ITEMS ARE RANKED, THEN ASK: "In view of those cost factors, does this change in any way your ranking of items in Column B-- the areas which definitely need changing before you'd consider staying here? _____

_____

15. How much would you be willing to pay on a monthly basis--either in rent or in payments--to obtain suitable housing for you and your family?

$_____per month
B41,42 ___ ___

16. I'm aware of the fact that cable TV is presently available at a cost of $6 per month. What monthly fee would be acceptable if the cable system gave you a complete range of the programs you wanted to see?

$_____per month
B43 ___

17. And how much in local taxes would you be willing to pay annually to have more and better schools and teachers? (HAND CARD B)
B44 ___

1___ Less than $25		5___ $101 - $200
2___ $25 - $50		6___ $201 - $300
3___ $51 - $75		7___ $301 - $400
4___ $76 - $100		8___ Over $400

156

18. Before moving to this part of Wyoming, what city or town have you most enjoyed living in over the past ten years or so?

Town_____ State_____   B45,46 ___ ___

   18a. How would you describe (NAME OF TOWN IN Q. 18)--as a:

      1___large city?   4___village?   B47 ___
      2___small city?   ___rural
      3___small town?

   18b. How long did you live there? _____years   B48 ___

19. (HAND RESPONDENT CARD C) Compared with (TOWN MENTIONED IN Q. 18), I'd like you to rate (PRESENT OR NEAREST TOWN) on a list of services which I will read to you. Please use the number on that card which is most appropriate--1, 2, 3, 4, or 5. (READ EACH ITEM BELOW, a THROUGH s)

	Present services are much better (1)	Present services are better (2)	Both locations about the same (3)	Present services are poorer (4)	Present services are much poorer (5)	DK	Relates to Ques.	
a. Retail stores........................	___	___	___	___	___		20	B49 ___
b. Medical and mental health services....	___	___	___	___	___		21	B50 ___
c. Local sanitation services (sewer, garbage collection).................	___	___	___	___	___		22	B51 ___
d. Availability of the TV programs you like to watch.....................	___	___	___	___	___		23	B52 ___
e. Other recreational facilities such as theaters, bowling alleys, tennis courts, etc........................	___	___	___	___	___		24	B53 ___
f. Public transportation to other locations.............................	___	___	___	___	___		25	B54 ___
g. Friendliness and acceptance into the community..........................	___	___	___	___	___		26	B55 ___
h. As a place to raise children.........	___	___	___	___	___		27	B56 ___
i. Suitable housing for your family's needs...............................	___	___	___	___	___			B57 ___
j. More and better schools and teachers..	___	___	___	___	___			B58 ___
k. Road and street maintenance..........	___	___	___	___	___			B59 ___
l. Local police protection.............	___	___	___	___	___			B60 ___
m. Local fire protection...............	___	___	___	___	___			B61 ___
n. Community planning...................	___	___	___	___	___			B62 ___
o. Parks................................	___	___	___	___	___			B63 ___
p. Responsiveness of local government....	___	___	___	___	___			B64 ___
q. Reasonable cost of living............	___	___	___	___	___			B65 ___
r. Financial services such as obtaining credit, savings programs, etc.......	___	___	___	___	___			B66 ___
s. Outdoor recreation...................	___	___	___	___	___			B67 ___

20. RETAIL STORES (a): Specifically, what kind of retail stores which are
presently missing or inadequate would you like to see in this community?
(FOR EACH TYPE, ASK:)

20a. Can you give me an example of a specific store you have in mind?

Type of Retail Establishment   Name of Store

_____   _____   B68,69 ___ ___

_____   _____   B70,71 ___ ___

_____   _____   B72,73 ___ ___

_____   _____   B74,75 ___ ___

21. MEDICAL AND MENTAL HEALTH FACILITIES (b): How do the local medical   B76 ___
and mental health care facilities need to be improved?   B77 _2_

                                                                      B78-80 ___ ___ ___

_____

END DECK TWO
_____

DECK THREE

(2 MENTIONS)
C1,2 ___ ___
C3,4 ___ ___

22. LOCAL SANITATION SERVICES (c): How could the local sanitation services
be upgraded?   (2 MENTIONS)

                                                                      C5,6 ___ ___

                                                                      C7,8 ___ ___

23. AVAILABILITY OF TV PROGRAMS (d): What kinds of TV programs would you
like to see more of? (FOR EACH TYPE ASK:)

23a. Can you give me an example?   (2 MENTIONS)

Type of Program   Example

_____   _____   C9,10 ___ ___

_____   _____   C11,12 ___ ___

_____   _____

23b.　How about local radio? Are there specific kinds of programs or
types of music which you'd like to see local radio stations provide?

(2 MENTIONS)

C13,14 ___ ___

C15,16 ___ ___

_____

_____

_____

_____

24. OTHER RECREATIONAL FACILITIES (e): Specifically, what additional or
improved recreational facilities would you like to see in the community?

(3 MENTIONS)

C17,18 ___ ___

C19,20 ___ ___

C21,22 ___ ___

_____

_____

_____

25. PUBLIC TRANSPORTATION (f): How would you suggest improving public
transportation facilities?

(2 MENTIONS)

C23,24 ___ ___

C25,26 ___ ___

26. FRIENDLINESS AND ACCEPTANCE (g): Can you think of any ways in which
a greater feeling of friendliness and acceptance could be promoted
in the community?

(2 MENTIONS)

C27,28 ___ ___

C29,30 ___ ___

159

26a. Some people have suggested introducing programs such as Welcome
Wagon or a referral service where you could telephone to get
basic information about where to go for things in the community--
such as medical attention, items you may need, etc. What is
your reaction to those suggestions? (INTERVIEWER RATE:

	Welcome Wagon	Referral Service
1. Respondent very enthusiastic	____	____
2. Respondent enthusiastic	____	____
3. Respondent lukewarm	____	____
4. Respondent regards it as unnecessary	____	____
5. Respondent regards it negatively	____	____
6. Cannot rate	____	____

C31 ___

C32 ___

27. AS A PLACE TO RAISE KIDS (h): What do you see as the greatest problems of raising children around here?

(2 MENTIONS)

C33,34 ___ ___

C35,36 ___ ___

27a. Is the problem greater for high school age or elementary school
age kids?
1___ Greater for high school age
2___ Greater for elementary school age
3___ Equally severe for both
4___ Don't know

C37 ___

27b. How would you suggest making this a better environment in which
to raise children?

(2 MENTIONS)

C38,39 ___ ___

C40,41 ___ ___

160

28. In your opinion, is (NAME OF TOWN OR NEAREST TOWN) a man's community
or a woman's community? That is, does this community offer a more
satisfying life to men or to women? Or is it the same for both?

    1___ More satisfying to men   C42 ___
    2___ More satisfying to women
    3___ The same for both--equally unsatisfying to both
    4___ The same for both--equally satisfying to both
    5___ Don't know

    IF ANSWER IS 1, 2 OR 3:

    28a. You've indicated that (this is more of man's/woman's community;
    the community is unsatisfactory for both men and women). What
    kinds of problems does this create? (PROBE)   (2 MENTIONS)

                                                                     C43,44 ___ ___

                                                                     C45,46 ___ ___

    28b. How would you suggest tackling that problem?   (2 MENTIONS)

                                                                     C47,48 ___ ___

                                                                     C49,50 ___ ___

29. How long do you expect to live in this part of Wyoming? ____years   C51 ___

    29a. Why is that?   (2 MENTIONS)

                                                                     C52,53 ___ ___

                                                                     C54,55 ___ ___

LET'S TALK FOR A MOMENT ABOUT YOUR PRESENT RESIDENCE...

               30. INTERVIEWER RECORD: 1___ Single family house   C56 ___
                                         2___ Apartment
                                         3___ Townhouse/condominium
                                         4___ Trailer
                                         5___ Other (specify)_____

31. How long have you lived in your present home?

    1___ Under 1 year   5___ 4-4.9 years   C57 ___
    2___ 1-1.9 years   6___ 5-9.9 years
    3___ 2-2.9 years   7___ 10 years or more
    4___ 3-3.9 years   8___ Don't know

161

32. Do you own or rent this (house, unit)? 1___Own   2___Rent   C58 ___

33. How many rooms are used for sleeping?

    (CIRCLE ONE)   1   2   3   4   5 or more   C59 ___

34. And how many bathrooms do you have?

    (CIRCLE ONE)   1   2   3 or more   C60 ___

    IF OWNED: 35. When did you buy this home? ____Month ____Year   C61 ___

               35a. How much did the home cost at the time you purchased
                     it?
                          $_____   C62,63 ___ ___

               35b. And how much are your monthly payments?

                          $_____per month   C64,65 ___ ___

    IF RENTED: 36. And what do you have to pay in rent here each month?

                          $_____per month   C66,67 ___ ___

    IF MOBILE HOME: 37. Have you ever lived in permanent housing since
                          coming to this part of Wyoming?

                          1___Yes   2___No   C68 ___

38. What do you see as the particular advantages or positive aspects of
    living in your present home? (PROBE)   (2 MENTIONS)

                                                                       C69,70 ___ ___

                                                                       C71,72 ___ ___

39. Is there anything you dislike about your present home? (PROBE)   (2 MENTIONS)

                                                                       C73,74 ___ ___

                                                                       C75,76 ___ ___

                                                                       C77 _3_

                                                                  C78-80 ___ ___ ___

                                                                  END DECK THREE

162

40. How much trouble did you have finding suitable housing when you first looked? (PROBE)

    40a. Was this your first choice of available housing when you were looking?

            1___Yes   2___No   D7 ___

        40b. Did you have any choice between permanent housing or a mobile home when you were looking?

                1___Could have had permanent housing   D8 ___
                2___Could have had mobile home
                3___Could have had neither

41. Let's talk for a moment about the kind of home and neighborhood you would like to live in now. As you know, it's possible that there will be a number of new housing units being built in the next few years. If such housing became available, could you describe to a developer in as much detail as possible the kind of home and neighborhood you would like to be living in here. Be realistic in terms of what you could afford at this time--recognizing that housing loans can probably be obtained for an amount twice that of your annual income. (RECORD VERBATIM DESCRIPTION)

RESPONDENT MENTIONED:

a___Own	j___Walking access to other needed facilities	D15 ___
b___Rent		D16 ___
c___Permanent housing	k___Grass	D17 ___
d___Mobile home	l___Trees	D18 ___
e___Single family home	m___Yard	D19 ___
f___Apartment	n___Garden	D20 ___
g___Townhouse/condominium	o___Paved streets, curbs & sidewalks	D21 ___
h___Close to work	p___Water and sewage facilities	D22 ___
i___Walking access to schools	q___Garage	

41a. Number of bedrooms needed: _____   D23 ___

41b. Number of bathrooms needed: _____   D24 ___

163

41c. If such a home were available to you, what would you regard as a reasonable price to pay?

IF OWN: $_____monthly payments   D25,26 ___ ___

IF RENT: $_____per month   D27,28 ___ ___

41d. And how far would you be willing to commute to live in such a home?

   _____miles   D29 ___

41e. If such housing were available to you, what are the chances of your remaining in this part of Wyoming? Would you say that the chances were:

    1___Excellent   D30 ___
    2___Good
    3___50-50
    4___Slim
    5___Poor

IF "SLIM" OR "POOR": 41f. Why would your chances of staying (2 MENTIONS)
          here be (SLIM, POOR) if suitable
          housing were available? D31 ___

                     D32 ___

41g. And if the type of home you described were not available, would you say that your chances of staying in this part of Wyoming were:

    1___Excellent   D33 ___
    2___Good
    3___50-50
    4___Slim
    5___Poor

42. Here are some pictures of various types of housing which might be available around here in several years. Study each one for a moment and then tell me which one you regard as most suitable for your family?

   _____   D34 ___

42a. Why do you regard that as most suitable? (3 MENTIONS)

                     D35,36 ___ ___

                     D37,38 ___ ___

                     D39,40 ___ ___

43. And which type of housing is least suitable for your family? _____

   43a. Why do you consider that to be least suitable?

D41 ___

(3 MENTIONS)

D42,43 ___ ___

D44,45 ___ ___

D46,47 ___ ___

44. (HAND CARD D) How would you rate each of the types of housing pictured on those cards? Let's first take Type A. Would you regard it
as (READ CHOICES LISTED BELOW AND REPEAT FOR EACH TYPE)

	Extremely Desirable (1)	Quite Desirable (2)	Tolerable (3)	Less than Desirable (4)	Extremely Undesirable (5)	
Type A	___	___	___	___	___	D48 ___
Type B	___	___	___	___	___	D49 ___
Type C	___	___	___	___	___	D50 ___
Type D	___	___	___	___	___	D51 ___
Type E	___	___	___	___	___	D52 ___
Type F	___	___	___	___	___	D53 ___

45. Now I'm going to read you some descriptions of types of families and
people. As I read each one, tell me how well you think the description fits you or your family. (HAND CARD E)

	Fits Very Well (1)	Describes Somewhat (2)	Does Not Fit Too Well (3)	Not At All Applicable (4)	
a. Likes to socialize a lot with the neighbors.	___	___	___	___	D54 ___
b. The type of person who gets deeply involved in community affairs.	___	___	___	___	D55 ___
c. Don't like to be tied down too long to one spot.	___	___	___	___	D56 ___
d. Likes to go out a lot and have a good time.	___	___	___	___	D57 ___
e. Prefers not to mix too much with the neighbors.	___	___	___	___	D58 ___
f. Enjoys having lots of children playing close by in the neighborhood.	___	___	___	___	D59 ___

165

46. Where do you go for most of your services and shopping--such as:

	Community	Distance from Home in Miles	
(1) Groceries	_____	_____	D60___ D61___
(2) Basic clothing for family	_____	_____	D62___ D63___
(3) Banking	_____	_____	D64___ D65___
(4) Health care	_____	_____	D66___ D67___

IF INDIVIDUAL LIVES MORE THAN THREE MILES FROM TOWN:

46a. Do you prefer to live as far as you do from some of the facilities we've just been discussing?

1___Yes   2___No   3___Don't know   D68 ____

(2 MENTIONS)

IF YES: 46b. Why is that?

D69,70 ___ ___

D71,72 ___ ___

IF NO: 46c. Why do you then?

(2 MENTIONS)

D73___
D74___

D75 ___
D76 ___
D77 ⎡4⎤
D78-80 ___ ___ ___

END DECK FOUR

47. Are there any colleges or facilities for adult education in this area?

1___Yes   2___No   3___Don't know

IF YES: 47a. What are they?_____

_____

DECK FIVE

E1 ___
(2 MENTIONS)

E2___

E3 ___

166

48. How much interest would you have in taking college level, vocational or adult education, courses? Would you say that you would be: (READ CHOICES)

        1___ Extremely interested
        2___ Quite interested
        3___ Fairly interested, or
        4___ Not at all interested
        ___ Don't know

E4 ___

IF (1) OR (2) TO Q. 48:   48a. What conditions might make it diffi-
                         cult to attend such courses, provided
                         they were available?

(2 MENTIONS)

E5 ___

E6 ___

FOR MALE RESPONDENTS:

49. (HAND RESPONDENT CARD F AND ASK:) In which of the employment or occupational categories on that card would you classify yourself? Read
all of the categories listed before answering.

01___ Presently employed in trona mining or processing.

E7,8 ___ ___

02___ Former mining employee presently employed on construction of
      trona plant.

E9,10 ___ ___

03___ Former mining employee presently employed on construction of the
      Jim Bridger plant.
04___ Former mining employee presently employed in some other construc-
      tion activity.
05___ Career construction employee presently employed on construction of
      trona plant.
06___ Career construction employee presently employed on construction of
      Jim Bridger plant.
07___ Career construction employee presently employed in some other
      construction activity.
08___ Presently employed on construction of trona plant, but formerly
      employed in some other field than mining or construction.
09___ Presently employed on construction of Jim Bridger plant, but
      formerly employed in some field other than mining or construction.
10___ Presently employed in construction other than trona or Jim Bridger
      plant but formerly employed in some field other than mining or
      construction.
11___ Employed in some field other than mining or construction.
12___ Unemployed ex-construction employee.
13___ Unemployed ex-mining employee.
14___ Unemployed (general).
15___ Retired.
16___ Other.

        IF NO. 11 IS CHECKED: 49a. What is your occupation? (GET SPECIFIC
                              DESCRIPTION OF DUTIES)_____

                    _____

                    _____

167

IF CATEGORIES 02-10 ARE INDICATED, ASK Q. 50:

50. If construction activity were to tail off around here and you were laid off, what would you be most likely to do to find employment?

        1___Seek local employment in mining.   E11 ___
        2___Seek other local employment.
        3___Seek construction employment in some other location.
        4___Seek other employment in some other location.
        5___Other (specify)_____

        6___Don't know

ASK ALL EMPLOYED RESPONDENTS Q. 51-51b:

51. How long have you been employed in this job?

      _____months or _____years   E12 ___

    51a. How long, in your estimation, will your present employment continue?
          _____months or _____years   E13 ___

    IF APPROPRIATE: 51b. Why would you expect it to end?   (2 MENTIONS)

                                                   E14,15 ___ ___

                                                   E16,17 ___ ___

52. Do you have any other occupational skills which you are not utilizing at present?
          1___Yes   2___No   3___Don't know   E18 ___

    IF YES: 52a. What are they?_____ (2 MENTIONS)
                                                  E19,20 ___ ___
                                                  E21,22 ___ ___

53. Is your wife presently employed?   1___Yes   2___No   E23 ___

54. And what is her occupation?_____ E24,25 ___ ___

    IF EMPLOYED:

55. Can you tell me exactly what her duties involve?   E26,27 ___ ___

56. And where is she employed?_____ E28,29 ___ ___

57. Does she have any other occupational skills which are not being
    utilized at present?

                    1__Yes   2__No   3__Don't know E30 ___

    IF YES: 57a. What are they? (2 MENTIONS)

                                                                                         E31,32 ___ ___

                                                                                   E33,34 ___ ___

58. How many minutes does it take you (and wife) to get to work each day?

          a. Male   _____minutes E35 ___

          b. Female _____minutes E36 ___

59. In terms of the work you're best qualified to do, are you doing as well
    here as you could somewhere else? First... (HAND CARD G)

	(1) Doing Better Here	(2) Doing as Well Here As Anywhere Else	(3) Could Do Better Somewhere Else	(4) Not Sure	
a. financially?	___	___	___	___	E37 ___
b. Chance to get ahead.	___	___	___	___	E38 ___
c. Chance to take advantage of your skills and abilities.	___	___	___	___	E39 ___
d. Gives you a sense of ac-complishment.	___	___	___	___	E40 ___

IF (3) IS CHECKED IN ANY ABOVE:

59e. Where do you feel you could do better?_____ E41,42 ___ ___

_____

60. In your opinion, how long will the present boom in mining and con-
    struction continue?

                       _____years E43 ___

    60a. If it dies out in the near future, would you expect to leave
    this area?

                1__Yes   2__No   3__Don't know E44 ___

60b. Based on recent market forecasts, it looks like the boom will continue for another 15 to 30 years. Therefore, if the boom continues
as expected, would you expect to leave the area?

      1___Yes   2___No   3___Don't know   E45 ___

    IF YES TO Q. 60b: 60c. Why would you leave?   (2 MENTIONS)

                                                      E46,47 ___ ___

                                                      E48,49 ___ ___

61. What was the last grade which you completed in school?

___Less than 8th grade	___1 year of college	E50 ___
___8th grade	___2 years of college	
___9th grade	___3 years of college	
___10th grade	___4 years of college	
___11th grade	(graduate)	
___12th grade (high school graduate)	___Post graduate	

62. For classification purposes only, we need to know your total family
income in 1973. Will you look at this card (HAND RESPONDENT CARD H)
and tell me which letter best represents your total family income in
1973 before taxes?

1___ A Less than $5,000	6___ F $15,000-$19,999	E51 ___
2___ B $5,000-$7,499	7___ G $20,000-$24,999	
3___ C $7,500-$9,999	8___ H $25,000 and over	
4___ D $10,000-$12,499	9___ Refused	
5___ E $12,500-$14,999	___ Don't know	

(FOR WOMEN ONLY) On Monday evening, September 23, and Tuesday morn-
ing September 24, we're planning to hold group discussions on the
subject of what can be done to make the life around here more enjoyable. We're paying individuals $10 apiece to participate for
about an hour. Would you be willing to sit in on one of those discussions?

1___Enthusiastic yes-Monday	5___Don't know	E52 ___
2___Enthusiastic yes-Tuesday	6___Not interested	
3___Qualified yes-Monday		
4___Qualified yes-Tuesday		

IF 1, 2, OR 3 TO Q. 63: 63a. Do you have access to an automobile?

1__Yes 2__No 3__Don't know   E53 __

63b. I'll need to know your name, address, and telephone number, so that we can contact you next week.

Name_____

Address_____

Telephone Number_____

64. (HAND RESPONDENT GREEN SHEET) We're very interested in knowing how people around here spend their leisure time and also how they would spend it, if the time and opportunity for certain activities were available.

Here is a list of various activities. On the left side of the page I'd like you to circle the number that tells how often you do those things now, using the guide at the top of the column. Then, on the right side of the page circle the number that tells how well you like doing those things, or think you would like doing it, if you had the chance. Use the guide at the top of the right hand column. Try not to skip any item. (LEAVE WITH RESPONDENT, BUT RETURN WITHIN TWO HOURS)

RECORD BUT DO NOT ASK:

65. Sex: 1__Female   2__Male   E54 __

66. Location: 01__Within city limits of Rock Springs   E55 __
                02__Within city limits of Green River
                03__Within city limits of Superior
                04__Within city limits of Reliance
                05__Within city limits of Point of Rocks
                06__Fringe (outside city limits, but within 3 miles of
                        Rock Springs)
                07__Fringe (outside city limits, but within 3 miles of
                        Green River)
                08__Fringe (outside city limits, but within 3 miles of
                        Superior)
                09__Fringe (outside city limits, but within 3 miles of
                        Reliance)
                10__Fringe (outside city limits, but within 3 miles of
                        Point of Rocks)
                11__Rural

67. Address_____

68. Name of Interviewer_____

69. Date_____

70. Time of completion of interview: _____AM or PM

	A	B	C
	(Rank top five 1 to 5 and bottom three as 13)	(Check those which need improvement before you would consider remaining in this community)	(Five most costly problems to solve)	DECK TWO
a. Retail stores....................................	_____	_____	_____	B1 _____ B2 _____ B3 _____
b. Medical and mental health services.............	_____	_____	_____	B4 _____ B5 _____ B6 _____
c. Suitable housing for your family's needs.......	_____	_____	_____	B7 _____ B8 _____ B9 _____
d. More and better schools and teachers...........	_____	_____	_____	B10 _____ B11 _____ B12 _____
e. Road and street maintenance....................	_____	_____	_____	B13 _____ B14 _____ B15 _____
f. Local police protection........................	_____	_____	_____	B16 _____ B17 _____ B18 _____
g. Local fire protection...........................	_____	_____	_____	B19 _____ B20 _____ B21 _____
h. Local sanitation services (sewer, garbage collection).....................................	_____	_____	_____	B22 _____ B23 _____ B24 _____
i. Community planning..............................	_____	_____	_____	B25 _____ B26 _____ B27 _____
j. Parks...	_____	_____	_____	B28 _____ B29 _____ B30 _____
k. Availability of the TV programs you like to watch...	_____	_____	_____	B31 _____ B32 _____ B33 _____
l. Outdoor recreation..............................	_____	_____	_____	B34 _____ B35 _____ B36 _____
m. Other recreational facilities such as theaters, bowling alleys, tennis courts,etc.	_____	_____	_____	B37 _____ B38 _____ B39 _____

LEISURE ACTIVITY CHECKLIST

<u>HOW OFTEN YOU DO THESE THINGS</u>

1. Two or three times a week or more
2. Once a week
3. Two or three times a month
4. Once a month
5. Less than once a month
6. Never do

<u>HOW WELL YOU LIKE OR THINK YOU</u>
<u>WOULD LIKE</u>

1. (Would) like very much
2. (Would) like
3. Indifferent
4. (Would) dislike
5. (Would) dislike very much

													Deck Six	
1	2	3	4	5	6	1. Individual art work (painting, sculpting)	1	2	3	4	5	F1 ___	F2 ___
1	2	3	4	5	6	2. Attending large social functions (dances, large parties, etc.)	1	2	3	4	5	F3 ___	F4 ___
1	2	3	4	5	6	3. Attending small social gatherings (small dinners, coffees, etc.)	1	2	3	4	5	F5 ___	F6 ___
1	2	3	4	5	6	4. Reading a book or magazine for pleasure	1	2	3	4	5	F7 ___	F8 ___
1	2	3	4	5	6	5. Playing cards or games with friends	1	2	3	4	5	F9 ___	F10 ___
1	2	3	4	5	6	6. Going to church	1	2	3	4	5	F11 ___	F12 ___
1	2	3	4	5	6	7. Going to a civic or community meeting	1	2	3	4	5	F13 ___	F14 ___
1	2	3	4	5	6	8. Going to a club/fraternal function	1	2	3	4	5	F15 ___	F16 ___
1	2	3	4	5	6	9. Visiting a neighbor or a friend	1	2	3	4	5	F17 ___	F18 ___
1	2	3	4	5	6	10. Entertaining at home	1	2	3	4	5	F19 ___	F20 ___
1	2	3	4	5	6	11. Working in local politics (on bond issues, for local candidates, etc.)	1	2	3	4	5	F21 ___	F22 ___
1	2	3	4	5	6	12. Bowling	1	2	3	4	5	F23 ___	F24 ___
1	2	3	4	5	6	13. Playing pool or billiards	1	2	3	4	5	F25 ___	F26 ___
1	2	3	4	5	6	14. Handball	1	2	3	4	5	F27 ___	F28 ___
1	2	3	4	5	6	15. Golf (in season)	1	2	3	4	5	F29 ___	F30 ___
1	2	3	4	5	6	16. Tennis (in season)	1	2	3	4	5	F31 ___	F32 ___
1	2	3	4	5	6	17. Swimming	1	2	3	4	5	F33 ___	F34 ___
1	2	3	4	5	6	18. Snow skiing (in season)	1	2	3	4	5	F35 ___	F36 ___
1	2	3	4	5	6	19. Snowmobiling (in season)	1	2	3	4	5	F37 ___	F38 ___
1	2	3	4	5	6	20. Ice skating (in season)	1	2	3	4	5	F39 ___	F40 ___
1	2	3	4	5	6	21. Hiking	1	2	3	4	5	F41 ___	F42 ___

1. Two or three times a week or more
2. Once a week
3. Two or three times a month
4. Once a month
5. Less than once a month
6. Never do

1. (Would) like very much
2. (Would) like
3. Indifferent
4. (Would) dislike
5. (Would) dislike very much

1 2 3 4 5 6		1 2 3 4 5	
1 2 3 4 5 6	22. Camping	1 2 3 4 5	F43 ___ F44 ___
1 2 3 4 5 6	23. Hunting (in season)	1 2 3 4 5	F45 ___ F46 ___
1 2 3 4 5 6	24. Fishing (in season)	1 2 3 4 5	F47 ___ F48 ___
1 2 3 4 5 6	25. Boating (in season)	1 2 3 4 5	F49 ___ F50 ___
1 2 3 4 5 6	26. Pistol, rifle, and shotgun shooting	1 2 3 4 5	F51 ___ F52 ___
1 2 3 4 5 6	27. Go to a movie	1 2 3 4 5	F53 ___ F54 ___
1 2 3 4 5 6	28. Go out to dinner	1 2 3 4 5	F55 ___ F56 ___
1 2 3 4 5 6	29. Go to a bar	1 2 3 4 5	F57 ___ F58 ___
1 2 3 4 5 6	30. Watch a high school sports event (in season)	1 2 3 4 5	F59 ___ F60 ___
1 2 3 4 5 6	31. Take classes in adult education	1 2 3 4 5	F61 ___ F62 ___
1 2 3 4 5 6	32. Play a team sport (softball, etc.)	1 2 3 4 5	F63 ___ F64 ___
1 2 3 4 5 6	33. Attend a symphony, concert or play	1 2 3 4 5	F65 ___ F66 ___
1 2 3 4 5 6	34. Roping, horseback riding and rodeoing	1 2 3 4 5	F67 ___ F68 ___
1 2 3 4 5 6	35. Visit a museum or art gallery	1 2 3 4 5	F69 ___ F70 ___
1 2 3 4 5 6	36. Gardening	1 2 3 4 5	F71 ___ F72 ___
1 2 3 4 5 6	37. Volunteer work--social service	1 2 3 4 5	F73 ___ F74 ___
1 2 3 4 5 6	38. Special hobbies (collecting, crafts, etc.)	1 2 3 4 5	F75 ___ F76 ___

Other activities (please specify)

_____

_____

_____

F77 _6_

F78-80 __ __ __

PICTURES OF TYPICAL SWEETWATER COUNTY, WYOMING HOUSING UNITS

EXAMPLE A

EXAMPLE B

EXAMPLE C

EXAMPLE D

EXAMPLE E

EXAMPLE F

177